WOMEN WHO
SURF

**French provocateur
Pauline Ado, suited up
and ready to rip**
Photo: Lucia Griggi

WOMEN WHO SURF

CHARGING WAVES WITH THE WORLD'S BEST

BEN MARCUS | LUCIA GRIGGI

FALCON®

GUILFORD, CONNECTICUT

An imprint of Globe Pequot
Falcon and FalconGuides are registered trademarks and Make Adventure Your Story
is a trademark of Rowman & Littlefield.

Distributed by NATIONAL BOOK NETWORK

Copyright © 2017 Rowman & Littlefield

All photos by Lucia Griggi unless otherwise noted

British Library Cataloguing-in-Publication Information available

Library of Congress Cataloging-in-Publication Data available

ISBN 978-1-4930-2485-8 (paperback)
ISBN 978-1-4930-2486-5 (e-book)

∞™ The paper used in this publication meets the minimum requirements of
American National Standard for Information Sciences—Permanence of Paper for
Printed Library Materials, ANSI/NISO Z39.48-1992.

Printed in the United States of America

The authors and Rowman & Littlefield assume no liability for accidents happening to,
or injuries sustained by, readers who engage in the activities described in this book.

CONTENTS

ACKNOWLEDGMENTS

Okay, it's 13:21 p.m. Hawaiian time on Saturday, December 17 and this book is almost *pau*—that means "done" in Hawaiian. I am upstairs at Kekoa Collective in Ward Center, across from my boat in Kewalo Basin. I just finished proofing this book on Dewey Doan's big iMac—because my Chromebook doesn't like Word (and neither do I really. Google Docs are the way to go). I would like to thank Dewey for the use of the office, and the computer, and the peace and quiet, and the chocolate-covered macadamia nuts.

This book is almost *pau* and that's a good feeling. There are a lot of people to thank.

Should I do that back to front, front to back or off the top of my head, stream-of-consciousness style?

Going back to front, thanks to Dewey Doan and his staff at Kekoa Collective. Thanks to Meredith Dias, Paulette Baker, David Legere, Sheryl Kober, Neil Cotterill, Melissa Evarts, and anyone else at Falcon Publishing involved in getting this book proofed, laid out, and done.

Of course, thanks to all of the women involved. All 17 of the women here cooperated in the writing and editing of their profiles. I am very, very careful when it comes to laying down people's lives, so thanks to all 17 of the women, but also Becky and Tom Hamilton for help with Bethany's profile and also Alana Blanchard's. Tami Gabeira for help with Maya Gabeira's profile, and also Carlos Burle and Rosaldo Cavalcanti and others who know Maya's story.

Thanks to Rochelle Ballard, Wrenna Delgado, Keala Kennelly, Andrea Moller, Leah Dawson, Mercedes Maidana, Easkey Britton, Bianca Valenti, Paige Alms, and Alison Teal for looking over their copy and making sure it was all accurate.

Special thanks to Martin Fitzgibbons for his help with Sally's profile. Very appreciated.

Also thanks to Peter Mel, Tara Mel, Shaun Tomson, and Nick Carroll for chiming in on Rosy Hodge, and also to Rosy for answering all those pesky emails. She's the busiest gal in show business.

Many thanks to Janet Macpherson for all she has done for a poor writer over the years. Hopefully her profile in this book is some kind of payback. Also thanks to Rachelle Hruska and Sean Macpherson for the family photos. And Jonette "Jonie" Mead in New Zealand for that Kiwi shot.

Thanks to Pauline Ado and David Bianic for their help with Pauline's profile.

A big thank you to the athletes who I interviewed that didn't make it into the book. My apologies, but there's always the second edition!

Thanks to Tonya Bickerton Watson, Chuck Gallagher (1934–2016), Duncan Norris, Jeff Nighswonger, Vanessa Siravo, Libby Defries, Cameron and Karen Farrer, and everyone else I forced the profiles on, and asked them to read them and give feedback.

Apologies to Lucia Griggi for blowing my top more than a few times on this book, and thanks to her for her photos and help with finding others. And that also goes for Sachi Cunningham, Elizabeth Pepin-Silva, Erik Aeder, Shannon Marie-Quirk, Fred Pompermayer, Martin Fitzgibbons, Tim McKenna, Sarah Lee, Mike Coots, Tony Heff, Dylan Gordon, Gary Miata, Red Bull, Ricardo Estevez, Anna Riedel, Bidu, Mike Bresnen, Jeff Munson, Jelle Mul, Waves of Freedom, Fitzgibbon International, and all of the photographers who contributed to this book.

I ran an Indiegogo to help raise money for the photo budget on this book, so thanks to Krickie McCooey, Dewey Doan (again), Gregg Brilliant, Rob Oliveros, Natasha Z, Cameron Farrer, R.J. Couture, Alexander Haro, Rachel Pettit, and Sarah Hauser for kicking in and helping to make this book POP!

Matt Luttrell is headed this way with $50 for another article I did. Thanks to him for his financial help.

Who am I leaving out of this? Who am I not thanking? Most likely, lots of people.

Thanks to L and L Hawaiian BBQ for letting me sit there hour after hour and work on this, and also Mike and Colleen at Snapper's Bar in Waikiki (sorry I was late yesterday) and all the bartenders and servers who kept me floating on club soda. This book took a looooooooong time to get done.

Thanks to the Hawaiian Islands, and of course, thanks to King Neptune for providing the waves you see in this book.

And apologies to everyone I am forgetting.

No words needed, Teahupoo
Photo: Tim McKenna

INTRODUCTION

In September 2011, Keala Kennelly was badly injured and nearly killed after a wipeout at Teahupoo—aka Chopes—an outer reef on the island of Tahiti that breaks with great vengeance and furious anger over unforgiving coral. Kennelly had successfully ridden giant waves during the famous Code Red swell on August 27. A few days later Kennelly was invited by Bruce Irons to surf in a special memorial heat for his brother Andy Irons during the Billabong Pro Men's World Championship Tour Event.

SOMETHING REALLY BAD

This was not a big day at Teahupoo, but as Kennelly explained to surfermag.com, Teahupoo is dangerous at any size: "That wave is so powerful from 2 to 20 feet. You are never really safe out there. There is always the possibility of something really bad happening."

On this day, something really bad happened. Kennelly got clipped by the lip on a just-overhead wave. Her face slammed into the reef; she came up bleeding, dazed and confused, and had to keep from panicking during a long rescue from the reef to the shore to an ambulance to the hospital in Papeete, in what must have been a very long, two-hour ride. Surgeons repaired the facial wounds, anesthetized her to remove pieces of coral embedded in her skull, and in the end placed sixty to eighty stitches in her face and ten in her skull.

This was a serious injury to a highly skilled surfer, and the shocking photos of Keala's reef-wracked face went around the world. If Kennelly never surfed Chopes again, no one would have blamed her. But two years later her facial scars had healed, and it was time to work on the mental damage.

Kennelly was ready to get back on the dragon that mauled her.

RETURN TO CHOPES

In May 2013 Keala returned to Teahupoo. "I came back and surfed the biggest waves at Chopes up until that point and got the best barrel of my life," Keala said in an e-mail. "I won the Women's Performance award at the XXL Big Wave awards that next year (2014)."

Two years after that—four years after her injury—in July 2015 Kennelly was back at Teahupoo on a day algebraically bigger and meaner than the day that nearly killed her. She flew to Tahiti, landed at 5 a.m., drove to the other side of the island, loaded her tow board into a kayak, and solo-paddled to the outer reef—hoping to take a rope from one of the established tow teams.

That's how Keala Kennelly rolls. She is gnar.

Kennelly travels on a wing and a prayer, with no set tow partner and no guarantee anyone will give her a shot. "I spent the entire day all geared up waiting for a turn with the tow rope," Kennelly told surfermag.com. "But skis were limited and the sets were inconsistent, so it was taking a long time for guys to get waves.

I waited all day. Finally, at the end of the day, Raimana [van Bastolaer, a Tahitian local] took a break and was nice enough to let me borrow his ski and driver."

After waiting all day and watching bomb after bomb unload on the reef—with surfers flinging themselves into death or glory rides—Kennelly was eager to get a bomb of her own before the sun set or the wind got too weird. And then she got one—and made history.

SWALLOWED

She remembered the time to surfermag.com:

I had to come into it real straight-on because when it sucks below sea level, it creates a trench that you don't want to come at sideways. If you do, you can catch a rail. Once I got through that trench, I bottom-turned up into the barrel and stuck my line. I was pretty determined to make it out of the barrel, but the wave turned mutant. The west bowl bent back at me at a 45-degree angle right as the bottom of the wave dropped out. It just swallowed me whole.

I got pinned on my back against the reef and was held there for a while. I came up and got a breath just in time to get the next wave on the head. It slammed me on the reef with so much force it blew my helmet off. The whole left side of my body hit really hard, and I felt like I broke my elbow and my hand. But after that wave I had so much adrenaline running through me, part of me wanted to go back out and get another one, but I was bleeding and in a lot of pain.

KEALA IS GNAR

Images of Kennelly's mutant Teahupoo wave went around the world just as the images of her smashed face did, and they caused a big sensation. She was nominated for the Pure Scot Best Barrel award of the annual World Surf League (WSL) XXL Big Wave Awards.

Keala dances with the dragon, tow surfing at Pe'ahi/Jaws on Maui
Photo: Erik Aeder

And on April 23, 2016, at The Grove in Anaheim, California, Kennelly accomplished what no other woman had done before: She won an XXL award in a category open to both men and women.

WORD FOR WORD

Kennelly took the stage to a lustful roar from the respectful crowd. Her speech was so heartfelt and good that it's worth repeating, word for word. Imagine these words, with Keala repeatedly interrupted by roars from the crowd and her own nervous, stoked giggles:

Wow. Wow. Wow, okay. This is really happening.

Well first I have to thank Raimana because he let me use his Jet Ski, and his driver.

And the good Lord knows you can't get a wave like that on your own. So. . . . They say, oh, behind every great man there's a great woman. But sometimes behind a great woman there's another great woman and I have . . . I have the most amazing extraordinary woman behind me and on my side. My partner, Nikki DiSanto. What I lack in sponsorship dollars, you make up for in your undying love and support. And I want to thank the entire DiSanto family for all your love and support and airline miles, because those came in way handy. And all my friends who are here tonight and all my friends and family who are watching back home. Especially my father, who taught me how to surf when I was a little girl.

Keala walking up to the podium at the 2016 XXL Big Wave Awards
Photo courtesy Ben Marcus

When I was a little girl, I didn't really want to be a little girl. Because when I was a little girl, I kept getting told you can't do that because you're a girl. You can't play football because you're a girl. You can't pee standing up because you're a girl. And for the record, I can pee standing up: Aim is another story, so I'm going to give you guys that one. But I heard all these things—you can't do this because you're a girl. You can't do this because you're a woman. Women can't surf. OK, women can surf, but women can't get barreled, women can't surf big waves, women can't surf Pipeline, women can't surf Chopes, women can't paddle Jaws, women can't get barreled at Jaws. So who I really, really, want to thank is everybody in my life who told me you can't do that because you're a woman, because that drove me to dedicate my life to proving you wrong. And it's been so damn FUN.

It's been so fun. Every time. A woman can't be nominated for a men's XXL award. A woman can't win a man's XXL award. I didn't even think it was possible, so I want to thank each and every one of you for sharing this moment with me right now when the impossible became possible, because I've never been so proud in my life to be a woman than I am tonight.

QUEEN BEE

A solid, heartfelt speech delivered with sincerity and passion and greeted with applause as thunderous as Teahupoo roaring forth. There is no question Keala Kennelly is the queen bee of women in serious surf. That Teahupoo barrel is undoubtedly the heaviest wave any woman has had to deal with, and the courage it took to tow into that thing four years after nearly losing her face on the reef—it's scarcely to be credited.

But Kennelly is also a poster girl for the trials and tribulations of being a woman surfer in the second decade of the twenty-first century. Keala is not sponsored by a big company, and usually she is winging it when surfing giant waves at Teahupoo, or Pe'ahi/Jaws on the island of Maui, or other big-wave spots in the Pacific and around the world. She is not in it for the money—although the $10,000 check she won for the Pure Scot Best Barrel must have made some amends.

WHAT'S WRONG WITH BEING SEXY?

Surfing is a sexy sport, but it's also a sexist sport. The bulk of the attention, fame, and money is focused on the men in small surf and large, competition and free surfing. There is a lot of debate in the surfing world regarding women selling themselves for their looks—how they can stuff themselves into wild bikinis—as opposed to how well they surf.

Woman have always struggled for equal acceptance in the macho world of surfing, and it took a macho woman like Keala Kennelly to break the boundaries and snatch an award from the men based on courage and skill.

> I want to thank each and every one of you for sharing this moment with me right now when the impossible became possible, because I've never been so proud in my life to be a woman than I am tonight.

Sarah Lee shooting Alison Teal on assignment in Fiji
Photo: Lucia Griggi

Keala's XXL award and speech came during a time when women's surfing is being elevated on all levels. From female-only surf schools around the world, to the women's WSL events getting prime-time coverage on the WSL webcasts, to women like Keala Kennelly, Paige Alms, Maya Gabeira, and a couple dozen other big-wave hell women pushing the limits in giant surf around the world.

Women's surfing has come a long way, baby, and Keala's Teahupoo wave, XXL award, and heartfelt speech represent a milestone and sign pointing to what is coming next for women who surf.

Lucia Griggi at work on assignment in the Pacific Ocean
Photo: Sarah Lee

I AM WOMAN, HEAR ME ROAR

Keala is not the only woman in this book who took, as surfers say, "dirty lickin's" and came back stronger. Almost all the women in *Women Who Surf* have suffered a variety of emotional, physical, and spiritual trauma: losing an arm to a tiger shark, nearly losing her face to the reef at Teahupoo, nearly drowning in Portugal, growing up homeschooled in New Jersey and the Himalayas. Broken boards, broken heads, broken homes, broken hearts.

And that goes for some of the women who photographed the women in this book: Lucia Griggi, Sachi Cunningham, and Sarah Lee. These women have all taken their lumps physically, financially, and equipment-wise to bring back the goods.

The women in this book are tough. They are surfers. They have overcome challenges and persevered. There are more out there, but here are profiles of 17 women who represent the many facets of women's surfing in the twenty-first century.

Rochelle Ballard, modeling her new line of bikinis
Photo: Mike Coots courtesy of Surf Into Yoga

Born: February 13, 1971
Birthplace: Montebello, California

KAUAI PRIDE

FORTY FIT

Rochelle Ballard is 45 years old now. She is still passionately surfing and charging, in the water as much now as when she was on tour, but "now it's just for the love of surfing and scoring the best waves I can on Kauai," Rochelle said.

Known for her fitness, flexibility, and toughness as a top pro in the 1990s, Rochelle is now leading Surf Into Yoga wellness retreats, staying healthy and strong into her 40s, while showing others how to stay healthy and strong from their 20s into their 60s.

In the 1990s, Rochelle was one of the pioneers of women proving themselves in big, hollow and powerful surf. She is tiny, she paid her dues and got knocked around like a rodeo clown, but she has left a large wake, which most of the women in this book are following to some degree.

ROOTS

Born Rochelle Gordines in Montebello, California, Rochelle moved with her parents to the island of Kauai when she was 6 months old. They moved her onto a Hawaiian island that was shrouded in secrecy at the time, protected with great vengeance and furious anger by local surfers who had seen what crowding had done to the vibe on Oahu and Maui, and practiced a sometimes violent form of island vigilantism to keep the outside world out.

Kauai has some of the best surf in the world, and the island is known for evolving very talented, very daring surfers: the Irons brothers, Keala Kennelly, Titus Kinimaka, Bethany Hamilton, Laird Hamilton, the Alexander brothers.

All of these Kauai surfers are known for talent and fearlessness in dangerous and giant surf.

Rochelle Ballard grew up mentored by Margo Oberg, a Californian and four-time world surfing champion in the 1960s, who moved to Kauai in 1972. Oberg is regarded as one of the pioneering women in big surf, and she passed the torch to Rochelle.

MARGO MENTOR

Regarding Margo Oberg: "I really admired her big wave surfing," said Rochelle in Christina Lessa's book *Women Who Win*.

> She received so much respect for what she did. She took me out surfing quite a bit one year, spent time with me, gave me pointers, and encouraged me to brave larger waves. I developed a love for surfing, a love that is almost impossible to express. There's an energy in the water that gives you every kind of feeling: peace, excitement, fear, a huge adrenaline rush, discouragement, frustration. The nature of surfing is such that you can't control the waves. You have to flow with them and find the rhythm of the ocean in order to work with it and experience what the ocean has to offer. Surfing is an art—we draw a new line on each wave we ride. It's also a science. You need to study the patterns of the ocean. And it's an ongoing lesson, because every few hours, the tides completely change.

Rochelle tips her sun visor to Margo, but she says her real influences came from her friendships and mentorships with the Kauai Boys, an archipelago of rascals who encourage fearlessness in big and gnarly surf: "They taught me how to ride the barrel and how to charge when I was usually the only girl out unless Keala or Mahina Alexander came out to surf with me."

Rochelle competed in local Kauai contests, then Hawaiian state contests, then national, and then the World Amateur Titles where she placed fourth in the World in 1988 and 1990. She turned professional in 1991 and finished 15th overall. She then married surfer and videographer Bill Ballard.

SUPER TUBER

In 1997 Rochelle won the World Qualifying Series, but it was a heat against Layne Beachley at the Billabong Pro at Burleigh Head, Queensland, that let people know the times were a-changin'. Rochelle scored two perfect 10s for riding in the barrel in her semifinal against Beachley—a record that still stands, 20 years later.

Writing in *The Encyclopedia of Surfing*, Matt Warshaw summed up Ballard as a competitor, but more importantly, as a charger who led the other women deeper into the barrel:

> In 1997 she won the World Qualifying Series tour, and the next year finished #4 on the world tour circuit. From 1993 to 2001 Ballard won eight circuit events; each year from 1996 to 1999 she finished runner-up to four-time world champion Lisa Andersen in the annual Surfer Magazine Readers Poll Awards

Warshaw went on to explain that Ballard's "surf world stature had little to do with contest results and everything to do with her groundbreaking performances in the hollow, hard-breaking waves." She dominated at places like Lance's Rights in the Mentawais and Backdoor Pipeline in Hawaii. "The tiny but hyper-fit Ballard (5'1", 105 pounds) wasn't the first woman surfer to ride inside the tube, but she was the first to do so habitually."

> Always a gutsy surfer, by the late '90s she'd added finesse and style to her repertoire, and was able to adjust her speed from behind the curl, weaving from one hollow section to the next. It was rare to see a woman riding the tube in 1995; five years later the top females were all competent, and in some cases first-rate tuberiders.

As surf journalist Gina Mackin wrote in 2000, "Ballard was the spark that touched off the women's tube revolution." Rochelle won the Surfer Poll Award for Most Popular Woman Surfer in 2000, 2001, and 2002, and finished the 2004 ASP World Tour season ranked second.

Three years later, at age 36, she left the tour.

BLUE CRUSHED

Rochelle starred in a long string of surf movies made by her husband Bill. But she also went Hollywood. If you saw the 2002 Hollywood "waxploitation" movie *Blue Crush*, that was Rochelle doubling for Kate Bosworth.

That shoot nearly ended Rochelle's career. While filming a scene where she and Hawaiian surfer Chris Taloa rode a wave together, the two collided, and Taloa's hard Hawaiian *okole* (behind) nearly paralyzed Rochelle.

"That was a heavy, heavy thing," Ballard was quoted in *The Surfer's Journal*, referring to the situation (and not Taloa's hard butt).

> . . . went from the most excruciating pain to total numbness. My left arm went limp. They took me out on the ski and then medivaced me to the hospital, and for a while there I thought I was paralyzed and would never surf again.
>
> I had what's called a "stinger": temporary paralysis and a few weeks recovery as I endured through it. I continued filming after a few days off from the set, but that just happened to be when they filmed the competition day at Pipeline with the perfect ride.

**Rochelle Ballard showing
her Backdoor skills**
Photos: Tony Heff

The Price of Gas continues: "Along with nearly breaking her neck, that almost broke her heart. Rochelle was none too happy to get beached for the controlled stunt shoot at Pipeline for the final scene, where Kate Bosworth's character surfs a Pipeline heat against Keala Kennelly. Four days after Ballard was injured, Pipeline was perfect for the Mike Stewart International Pipeline Pro 2002. When the contest ended, the movie had exactly one hour of perfect Pipeline to capture the climactic last ride of the movie where Anne Marie faces her fears and charges Pipeline for death or glory.

Ballard saw the perfect Pipeline she had been jonesing for, but discretion was the better part of valor: John Stockwell, the film's director, and Brian Keaulana, the water safety supervisor, asked her if she could do it, but Ballard had to decline. "That was the worst feeling of my life, but I was too messed up physically to go charge giant Pipe backside."

With their #1 stunt person sidelined, the producers put Hawaiian surfer Noah Johnson in a women's swimsuit and a contest singlet, and he did the surfing for the finale of *Blue Crush.*

THE PERILS OF ROCHELLE

Rochelle was bummed to miss out on surfing perfect Pipeline with one other person (for stunt pay), and also make Hollywood history, but that incident on the set of *Blue Crush* was far from her only, or worst, surfing injury. When she tried tow surfing in Tahiti, weighing just 109 pounds and without the right equipment, she nearly drowned.

Rochelle seems like the kind of charging adrenaline junkie who would get into tow surfing. But while being small, super-fit and quick is an advantage in some kinds of surf, lightness is actually a drawback in tow surfing, where some heft and weight is needed to deal with the stresses of speed, wind and chops, and everything else coming at a surfer who is being whipped into a 15- to 40-foot wave at 30 miles per hour. After a couple of bad experiences, she decided, "I'd rather put my energy into riding Pipeline and really quality barrel riding as my commitment to powerful surfing."

CHANGES

In 2004, Rochelle retired from professional surfing at age 36. Divorced from her husband, Bill, she spent most of her time on Kauai, staying fit with surfing and yoga, and leading Surf Into Yoga wellness retreats. "It seems like just a few years ago that I was on tour and in fact it has been nine years now—almost a decade."

Retired from pro surfing for nine years, now living comfortably and working hard on Kauai, Rochelle is surrounded by the beauty of the Garden Isle and enjoys every opportunity to go surfing.

She has rediscovered the passion she felt when she first started, enjoying surfing with her friends and trying to surf the best waves on the island. "It's more the quality of the wave than the size for me today."

"It's more the quality of the wave than the size for me today."

Rochelle leading her Surf Into Yoga wellness retreats
Photo: Mike Coots courtesy of Surf Into Yoga

Wrenna waiting for a wave at Himalayas, an outer reef spot on the North Shore of Oahu
Photo: Matt Paul

Born: October 10, 1998
Birthplace: A hospital on the Jersey Shore

JERSEY SHORE TO NORTH SHORE

JOISEY GOIL

Many of the women in this book have suffered a variety of traumas: emotional, physical, financial, or spiritual. Wrenna Delgado grew up being homeschooled in New Jersey, but she hasn't let it affect her performance. She has answered the siren call to ride the wild surf in Hawaii—and has never looked back. A near-death experience at Makaha in 2009 changed her approach to surfboards and safety equipment. In 2010 Wrenna paddled out at Mavericks for the first time, and in 2014 she was part of the WickrX Expression Session—a noncompetitive "expression session" that invited fifteen women to surf Mavericks and split a $55,000 purse.

Wrenna and a crew of women charged into some stormy, bumpy 15-foot surf at Mavericks—it wasn't easy, but Mavericks isn't supposed to be. More recently Wrenna and six other big-wave women paddled into triple-overhead surf on a North Shore outer reef for the Go Big Project—part of an ongoing video project that includes wingsuit flying, rally cars, and a lot of adrenal sports.

ROOTS

Wrenna is originally from Belmar, New Jersey, but moved about 5 miles south to Manasquan when she was 8 years old to escape a menacing neighbor. "He would clean his speargun pointed at my mom while she was breastfeeding on our porch," Wrenna remembered. "And this, my mom could not handle. So we moved.

Wrenna Delgado at Waimea Bay, about to hit the accelerator
Photo: Gary Miata courtesy Wrenna Delgado

My mom was very antiestablishment; she homeschooled us and kept us slightly on the fringe, and so I never really identified with one place as my home."

Wrenna's father, Miguel, is from the Canary Islands, so the family vacationed there every year and visited her grandparents. The Canary Islands are to the Atlantic what the Hawaiian Islands are to the Pacific: volcanic peaks that rise abruptly from out of the sea and cause open ocean swells to break with great fury. On those trips Wrenna's dad surfed with his friends and tried to convince her to go out with them, but as a young girl she wasn't ready yet: "I wasn't having it. Too scared."

HOMESCHOOL IS COOL

Wrenna's antiestablishment mom couldn't see sending Wrenna to a regular public school and mixing her with the general population. Instead she homeschooled. The schools in Wrenna's area didn't offer sports to homeschooled kids, so she went with a group of other homeschoolers to the park to play different sports. In the summers she competed in junior lifeguarding—swim races, beach runs, paddleboard races—which she loved. "I lived for that."

Wrenna started surfing at 15, which is a little late for a beach girl, but that's when she got into it, encouraged by her father and older brother. Her father was the only surf hero she had growing up: "It wasn't the fact that he surfed; I admired people who are ocean minded. People who NEED to get in the water every day. It doesn't matter what you're doing—surfing, swimming, diving—I love the ocean and all that it offers us."

Her first board was a bright yellow soft top, and she took to it pretty quickly. Because she was homeschooled, she had flextime, which she spent working and surfing. She worked mornings at a flower farm and afternoons at the local library, and on weekends she babysat. She and her best friend, Stephanie, another homeschooler, rode their bikes to the beach with their surfboards every chance they got. When they weren't surfing, they skateboarded around town "feeling free that we weren't in school but also like total outsiders for the same reason."

Summers are sublime along the Jersey Shore, but winters are harsh. By age 19 Wrenna had had enough of the Jersey yin and yang. She jumped on a big old jet airliner and headed west, across the continent and all the way to the Hawaiian Islands.

HERE TODAY, GONE TO OAHU

Remember that MTV video of the girl in the bee costume? She feels lonely and then sees all the other bees, runs through the gate, and dances around with them happily? That's Wrenna Delgado, finding herself on the North Shore. "The North Shore felt like and some ways still is a big playground. The ocean is always there, pulling you to it, it was a dream come true."

She lived in Waialua when she first got there. Make an "L" with your thumb and forefinger—palm side up. The tip of your thumb is Kaena Point, and about the middle of your thumb is Waialua, a still-quiet area that looks east, toward the North Shore. Waialua is far from the full-time hippy-groovy-tattooed-food-truck–surf-school-surf scene the North Shore has become since Y2K, and that suited Wrenna fine. She was so enamored of the freedom and beauty of the island and the culture that she was never scared or intimidated being in a new place. She threw herself into surfing, met some different people, and slowly found her groove. "I was overwhelmed by the reverence people have for the ocean and water sports. Finally, a place where the majority of people do something in the ocean and everyone respects that."

Wrenna is 6'2", super-fit with a lot of energy, but no matter how much energy a person might possess, the North Shore will soak it up and have energy to spare. Wrenna threw herself into the ocean life of the North Shore. She loved it. "I had a boyfriend at the time who introduced me to the underground big wave scene. Bonfires on the land with a rowdy group of older guys and their seemingly ethereal significant others. The North Shore did come off as a fairly male dominant area. Funny, though, that has changed since I've lived here."

"The North Shore felt like and some ways still is a big playground. The ocean is always there, pulling you to it, it was a dream come true."

Because of Wrenna's height and physical condition, going out in bigger surf came naturally to her. Two years after arriving, and six years after her first steps on a surfboard, Wrenna was in full swing on the North Shore, surfing big Waimea and some outer reefs. Season after season she went bigger and bigger. There are dozens of possible waves to surf along the Seven Mile Miracle of the North Shore—waves breaking on the beach, waves breaking a mile out to sea. Guided by her free-spirited mentor, Hawaiian surfer Sturmar Ahsing, Wrenna surfed them all. Her favorite is Himalayas, an outer reef that breaks way out to sea. "I love that wave; no matter how big it's breaking, I'd rather surf there than anywhere else."

Wrenna loves the freedom Hawaii has given her to be herself and be wild. She wouldn't change anything about the nine years she's been there. "Good experiences or bad, it's an experience nonetheless. It may sound a little woo-woo, but Hawaii has helped me heal, grow, and be at peace with my journey."

DANGERS

The North Shore isn't all fun and games. Shark attacks have become more common as the number of people in the water increases. And the waves there have injured and killed some of the most experienced surfers: Titus Kinimaka breaking his leg at Waimea Bay, Todd Chesser drowning at Outside Alligators, Donnie Solomon going over the falls at Waimea Bay and drowning.

Wrenna had a near-death experience the first time she surfed big Makaha in 2009. The first wave of an enormous set pushed her under, stripping off her swimsuit. After struggling to the surface, she was rolled by the next wave and had to be rescued by the Makaha lifeguards. "I've never been rolled by a wave like that. If I wasn't in a complete state of adrenaline/survival, I would have cried because it was so beautiful. . . . It was like seeing a wonder of the world and then to experience that power . . . surreal, terrifying."

Wrenna at the Women's expression session
Photo: Shannon Quirk

SAFETY CONSCIOUS

That near-death wipeout at Makaha injected some gravitas into Wrenna's big-wave philosophy, and her equipment and approach changed from there. "In the beginning I messed around with different boards—single fins, clunkers, narrow guns. I always thought the whole 'You're only as good as your equipment' was untrue; I thought it came down to the surfer." She started using thicker boards with a quad fin setup that had a good release once she got on the wave. A fuller outline in the nose helps her get in waves early, which she likes.

After having her swimsuit stripped at Makaha, Wrenna now wears one-piece wet suits that don't go anywhere when the going gets tough. And after swimming all those strokes to get to the surface, only to take #2 on the Gulliver, she has also embraced the new safety equipment that has emerged in the twenty-first century, including a safety vest. They didn't exist when Wrenna first started surfing, and she sees the value in having learned without one:

> I wear a safety vest. In the beginning I didn't because they didn't really exist yet. I'm glad I got to experience that. It was very good for me to start that way, having to survive the consequences fully. You lose your board, you swim in, no matter how far. If you don't swim in, chances are you're gone or about to have the craziest open-ocean experience of your life.

But she recognizes that equipment like vests can save your life. "I understand the old school [you're on your own] novelty. I admire that and respect it, but safety equipment has its time and place."

REVERSE PARACHUTE

Inflatable safety vests are a fairly recent development in big-wave surfing. There were various experiments after Y2K, but vests became legitimized after arguably the most accomplished big-wave surfer, Shane Dorian, nearly drowned at Mavericks in 2011. Getting pounded 30 feet down, worrying about the wife and kids was the mother of invention in Dorian's case, and he worked with Billabong to develop the Billabong V1 vest in 2011. The vest is equipped with pull tabs that inflate the vest and act like a reverse parachute, rocketing the drowning surfer to the surface for that blessed breath of air and saving a lot of physical wear and tear. Patagonia followed with an inflatable vest in 2012, and in 2014 Quiksilver partnered with French company Aqua Lung to make their own version. At the big-wave events at Jaws and Waimea during the winter of 2015–2016, almost all of the competitors were wearing vests.

In a Surfline.com article by Marcus Sanders, Peter Mel talked about the philosophy of the vests:

> The biggest thing for me is that you get worn out quickly if you're taking beatings, but having a vest doesn't make me less careful. There's still injuries that can happen: the bottom, your board . . .
>
> It's definitely something that's affected the lineup this year. There's guys pushing it over the ledge a little bit more knowing they have that backup, knowing they can get to the surface.

Wrenna has embraced the vest philosophy. In 2010 Kala Alexander handed her a wakeboarding vest and told her that he wouldn't allow her to surf if she didn't wear it. After a couple of sessions, she started to like it. She wears a padded vest in 12- to 15-foot waves and an inflatable in 15-plus. "What if you hit your head, you dislocate your shoulder, break a rib? You just don't know. I don't care if I look like an ass; I want to go home to my family."

JET SKIS TO THE RESCUE

The lifeguards on the North Shore were among the first to utilize personal watercraft (PWC) for heavy-water rescues, and they now have it down to an art. When you've just taken a beating to within an inch of your life, are a half mile out to sea, and your board is broken or missing—that rescue ski is a beautiful thing. Wrenna's been saved by a ski a few times herself, but she believes the best safety measure is to use your head and avoid using your ego as a motivator. "I know that you need a push every once in a while, but be smart. I play it safe a lot, which is why I'm not going after sponsors and pursuing the big-wave thing. I want to do this forever, so I'm doing it my way."

My Way. Like Sinatra. From Jersey.

BIG-WAVE WAHINE

Wrenna Delgado is a big-wave wahine at a time when opportunities are emerging for girls who like to go big. Keala Kennelly winning the Best Barrel at the 2015–2016 WSL XXL Big Wave Awards was a stepping-stone, and Wrenna has been involved in many projects putting women in front of giant surf. She's traveled to Jaws, Puerto Escondido, Mavericks, Nelscott Reef, and a bombie in Southern Australia. She surfed in the Nelscott Reef expression session for women, the WickrX session at Mavericks, and the Go Big project session. And her friend, director Claire Gorman, has been making a movie about her and Mercedes Maidana for the past few years.

THE FUTURE

As much as she misses pork roll egg-and-cheese sandwiches, killer hurricanes, and freezing to death in winter, Wrenna won't be headed back to New Jersey anytime soon. She and her family have a farm on the North Shore, where she wants to stay—and hopefully surf big waves—forever. "I want to travel and give my kids as many experiences as I can afford. I have lots of hopes and dreams. I guess we will see what happens when it does!"

SEPARATE AND EQUAL

In September 2016, as this book was being finished up, Wrenna Delgado called from the North Shore to ask for advice on establishing a women's big-wave event on the North Shore, at Waimea Bay. Wrenna felt the time was right; the talent and desire were there, and after working on this book and talking to all these big-wave women, that seemed to be the right call.

There are a lot of logistics, politics and personalities, and permits and expenses to deal with when setting up an event on the North Shore in winter, but Wrenna is determined. It will be an invitational contest including women from all over the world who have dedicated themselves to the thrill and sport of big-wave riding. Wrenna believes a women-only competition will be a huge step for the

In my opinion, there are many competent water women in and out of the spotlight who have been wanting and waiting for a chance to show what they are capable of. An event dedicated to women is the solution.

legitimacy of female big-wave surfing. Right now men and women don't have the same opportunities and resources in the big-wave realm, and it isn't fair to ask women to compete against men with more years in the water, more opportunity to travel, and more time honing their skills. Says Wrenna, "In my opinion, there are many competent water women in and out of the spotlight who have been wanting and waiting for a chance to show what they are capable of. An event dedicated to women is the solution."

CALL IT THE BETTY?

According to Wrenna, Waimea Bay would be the ideal location for such an event. Hawaii brought surfing to the world, and ancient Hawaiian women surfed alongside men. But not everyone agrees. Many people still don't see the importance of investing in women's big-wave surfing or the value in having equality among men and women, and they try to control the sport and stop forward momentum. Wrenna believes strongly in the contest now and for future generations, "for young women to aspire to follow their passion and dreams and not have to be 'one of the guys' in order to be accepted."

Bethany Hamilton on the North Shore, winter 2008
Photo: Lucia Griggi

BETHANY HAMILTON

Born: February 8, 1990
Birthplace: Lihue, Kauai

GOTTA HAVE FAITH

FAME

In late May 2016, Bethany Hamilton was on the Fijian island of Tavarua, competing in the women's division of the WSL Fiji Pro event. Her bouncing baby boy, Tobias, was there in the boat, and Bethany handed him off so she could jump overboard and take on solid, powerful, 6-foot reef break surf.

Bethany charged and made it to the semis, and drew high praise from none other than Kelly Slater. A phenomenal Cloudbreak surfer, Kelly bore witness to a phenomenon:

Anyone who isn't inspired by @bethanyhamilton and her physical attributes after losing her arm to a tiger shark in Kauai some years ago should check their pulse. The hardships she overcomes to perform at the level she does in the ocean is arguably unparalleled in men's or women's sport. It's nice she got a start in the @wsl#FijiPro this week and took down some big names in the process, just losing out in the semis to the eventual winner, @johannedefay. I hope to see her in more events this year, and hopefully she can requalify on just the strength of a few good results as a wildcard this year on tour. I think everyone should have a full surf with one arm strapped to their side and attempt not only to paddle out but put themselves in position at heavy spots like Pipe, Jaws, and Cloudbreak and try to get up on a short board. I'm scared to try it myself and ridiculously impressed with her talents. Congratulations on your third-place result at #Cloudbreak, @tavaruaislandresort. Great to watch you surf in those conditions.

What Kelly said is absolutely right. It's amazing what Bethany Hamilton has overcome and is able to do, with one arm, over a sharp, tropical reef in the middle of the Pacific. Paddling into the wind and chop and catching waves with one arm is amazing enough. But Bethany Hamilton is a goofy foot, which means she faces the wave going left, and she needs that back arm to drag into the wave face to slow down and spend more time in the barrel. She doesn't have that left arm, but she still racks up heaps of tube time.

She needs that left arm as a counterbalance for turns and cutbacks—she doesn't have it, but she shralped the faces at Fiji as well as any of the other women.

And then she kicked out, grabbed her board, paddled over to the PWC, grabbed the sled, and pulled herself onto the sled, all with one arm.

It's amazing. It's impossible. Bethany makes it happen.

Gotta have faith.

SHARK ATTACK!

The 2003 shark attack on Bethany Hamilton is a story that has been told many times, from tales told around a campfire on Kauai to a major Hollywood movie starring Helen Hunt and Dennis Quaid.

Bethany has told her shark story a thousand times in a variety of ways, but she tells the story in simple terms in her book *Soul Surfer: A True Story of Faith Family and Fighting to Get Back on the Board*:

It came, literally, out of the blue.

I had no warning at all; not even the slightest hint of danger on the horizon. The waves were small and inconsistent, and I was just kind of rolling along with them, relaxing on my board with my left arm dangling in the cool water. I remember thinking, "I hope the surf picks up soon. . . ."

That's all it took: a split second. I felt a lot of pressure and a couple of lightning fast tugs. Then I watched in shock as the water around me turned bright red. Somehow, I stayed calm. My left arm was gone almost to the armpit, along with a huge crescent-shaped chunk of my red, white, and blue surfboard. . . .

I remember most clearly what the Kauai paramedic said to me in the ambulance. He spoke softly and held my hand as we were pulling out of the beach parking lot. He whispered in my ear, "God will never leave you or forsake you." He was right.

ROOTS

On Halloween 2003 Bethany Hamilton was 13 years old and surf-stoked down to her DNA. She was born on Kauai, grew up there, and was being shaped by the same forces—oceanic, natural, spiritual, human—that had shaped great Kauai surfers like Laird Hamilton (no relation), the Irons brothers, Rochelle Ballard, Keala Kennelly, and Bethany's best friend, Alana Blanchard. "In May 2003 she won the women's division of a statewide event in Honolulu," Matt Warshaw wrote in *The Encyclopedia of Surfing*, "beating a field of mostly older competitors, at which point the thin blond goofy footer was touted as one of the island's hottest young pro tour prospects."

Five months after that Honolulu contest, on Halloween morning 2003, Bethany Hamilton was surfing with Alana Blanchard at a spot called Tunnels—aka Makua Beach—a popular snorkeling and surfing reef between Hanalei Bay and the Na Pali Coast.

The surf was small; the day was calm. Bethany was sitting there, minding her own business, thinking whatever a 13-year-old surf-stoked girl thinks about when confronted by the beauty of Kauai, when that tiger shark—estimated to be 13 feet long—bit her arm off.

Bethany was rescued by Alana Blanchard and Alana's father, Holt. He used a rash guard to make a tourniquet and was faced with the challenge of getting Bethany and everyone safely to shore.

Alerted that her daughter had been injured, Cheri Hamilton drove so fast from Hanalei toward Haena that cops pulled her over until the paramedics told them what was up. Cheri had enough to worry about that day: Her husband Tom was about to undergo surgery for a knee problem.

At the hospital, the operating doctor saw the clean bite and wondered if someone had performed an amputation on the young girl between the beach and the operating table. No one had. A tiger shark's bite is that surgical, that sharp, that complete.

THIRTEEN YEARS LATER

Thirteen years have passed since Bethany Hamilton had her arm taken by a tiger shark. As dramatic as that event was—and there are few human experiences more dramatic than being nearly eaten by a large animal—the drama had just begun.

Beyond the horror and pain, expense and inconvenience, and possible nightmares of having her arm taken clean off by a 1,500-pound shark, Bethany Hamilton was just a surf-stoked 13-year-old girl living in an earthly paradise, inspired by the nature and the ocean and the great surfers all around her. She just wanted to surf, as much and as well as possible, and now she was missing a crucial ingredient: her left arm. A left arm for paddling, dragging in the wave face so she could pull into the tube, and pushing down on the deck of the board so she could duck-dive under waves.

GOTTA HAVE FAITH

All that has come since the incident took faith, but Bethany Hamilton has never lacked for that, as she explained on the bethanyhamilton.com website:

> Growing up in a Christian home was a huge blessing for me. At a young age I was introduced to what Jesus Christ has done for all of mankind. . . . As rough times come my way, like when I lost my arm to the shark, and as life throws challenging curve balls, I take joy and am grounded in God's promises found in His Word, the Bible. I still hold fast to His truths today. One of my favorite verses is Ephesians 2:8–9:
>
> "For by grace you have been saved through faith. And this is not your own doing; it is the gift of God, not a result of works, so that no one may boast."

As rough times come my way, like when I lost my arm to the shark, and as life throws challenging curve balls, I take joy and am grounded in God's promises found in His Word, the Bible.

ONE MONTH LATER

It was faith and family that propelled Bethany's fast return. Some people who have been attacked by a shark might have moved to Montana. Not Bethany. She was back surfing within a month after the attack—one month!—using a board specially outfitted by her father with a handle that helped her "duck-dive" to get through waves. "Surfing again was all about rebalancing," Bethany's father, Tom, said. "Takes time . . . 95 percent practice."

Bethany's first surf was on a 9-foot Malibu [Australian term for longboard], which she needed for paddling speed and stability. Right away I noticed that she was pushing up on the outside right rail, which caused the board to tilt. So I told her to push up off the center stringer. She was determined to catch a wave by herself and wouldn't let me give her a push or shove from behind her as I did when she was a 5-year-old. She quickly worked her way downward in board size, only using the Malibu for a week or so. It was at that point that I worked with her shaper to outfit a special board with a handle which helped her duck-dive to get through waves.

SPECIAL GIRL

Seven months after the attack—that's right, *seven months*—Bethany competed at the 2004 National Scholastic Surfing Association Nationals at Lower Trestles and placed fifth in the Open Women's division.

Www.surfermag.com let the world know there were two phenomena bubbling in that division.

But the real story of Nationals was the emerging prowess of the women's competitors, [including] Kauai's Bethany Hamilton, who lost her left arm in a shark attack last October. Bethany not only made the final but surfed well, managing to pick off set waves and paddle for position. The winner of that heat, however, was 11-year-old Carissa Moore from Hawaii, who made Nationals history by winning the Open Women's, Explorer Women's, and Middle School Girls' divisions.

Bethany on the North Shore of Oahu
Photo: Lucia Griggi

One year later, Bethany won that NSSA Explorer Women's division in the nationals. With one arm. The official press release from the NSSA was effusive:

BETHANY DOES IT! Dismiss all the hype, brush aside the shark, forget about using only one arm. Fifteen-year-old Bethany Hamilton absolutely annihilated the Explorer Women's final, shredding Lowers lefts to pieces. Accepting her National title at the Banquet to a 500-person standing ovation, Bethany thanked God and her coach, Ben Aipa, for helping her on her title mission. After her third-place showing in the Open Women's division (before the attack) in 2003, we knew it was only a matter of time until this special girl achieved Nationals gold.

TIMELINE: 2004 TO 2015

The next thirteen years of Bethany's life were busy, busy, busy and impossible to condense into short form. For the whole story, go to bethanyhamilton.com/category/timeline. That timeline condenses down to thirteen years of travel, surf trips, awards, public speaking, TV shows, surfing competition, books, and a movie deal that led to the production of *Soul Surfer*, which hit theaters on April 8, 2011.

Bethany traveled around the United States, France, United Kingdom, and Ireland to promote the release of the movie, which was nominated for several awards—Teen Choice Movie Drama, Teen Choice Movie Actress Drama (AnnaSophia Robb), ESPY Best Sports Movie, Satellite Award for Best Music Score (Marco Beltrami), Artios Award in Casting Independent Features (Joey Paul Jensen), VH1's Do Something Awards—and won the ICM (Inspirational Country Music) Faith, Family & Country Award!

Bethany hitting it hard
Photo: Erik Aeder

Bethany's quiver on the North Shore
Photo: Lucia Griggi

Ten years after the shark attack, Bethany married youth minister Adam Dirks. Two years after that, she announced she was with child: a son. Tobias was born June 1, 2015, and seven months later (!), mom handed Tobias off to a babysitter so she could tow into some bombs at Pe'ahi.

TOWING JAWS

On January 4, 2016, Bethany towed into a few giant waves at Pe'ahi/Jaws on the island of Maui. Tow surfing is one aspect of surfing where having only one arm isn't a disadvantage, and Bethany handled the big, windy wave at Jaws with style.

The Internet was buzzing after that, but there were some naysayers who had the audacity to suggest that Bethany should paddle into Pe'ahi/Jaws—with one arm!

Both sides of Bethany on the North Shore
Photos: Lucia Griggi

Impossible, you say? Not according to Dear Old Dad Tom Hamilton: "Bethany got a call from a friend at Jaws who said it was good. Bethany checked it, and the surfers were all coming in and the windsurfers were going out. So she went out and paddled in because of a small crowd, which made it accessible compared to the regular sixty guys out."

SAFE AT HOME

During summer 2016, Bethany Hamilton competed at the Fiji Pro, made it to the semis, and inspired that comment from Kelly Slater. Kelly's thoughts were sincere and from the heart. He has seen a lot in his 40-something years, and it's hard to shock or impress him, but Kelly was shocked and awed by watching Bethany Hamilton surf Cloudbreak with one arm.

Bethany Hamilton tow surfing giant Pe'ahi/Jaws
Photos: Erik Aeder

Bethany's story is remarkable—an alchemy of faith, family, stoke, love. The traumatized 13-year-old has blossomed into a confident, happily married woman and mom who has seen the world—and the world has seen her—but she is happiest when she is surrounded by the beauty and quiet of Kauai and loves nothing more than to go surfing with her friend, Alana Blanchard.

All is well.

Eye of the tigress. Maya
Gabeira at Nazare.
Photo courtesy Red Bull

MAYA GABEIRA

Born: April 10, 1987
Birthplace: Rio de Janeiro, Brazil

SHE'S SO TOUGH

To me it's like, life gives you challenges and then you have to face them and you have to overcome them and you have to reassure what path you are on. . . . I feel strong now again, after a long time of feeling very fragile.

—*Maya Gabeira*

@MAYA

Let's take a look at Maya Gabeira's social media (@maya) and see what we can learn about her:

✦ She has more than 300,000 followers and many posts.

✦ Maya is an ocean-loving adrenaline junkie who loves to charge humongous waves and pull into the barrel on medium to large waves.

✦ You will see tributes to fallen or retired athletes or artists who have inspired her: Muhammad Ali, David Bowie, Kobe Bryant, Ayrton Senna, Brock Little.

✦ She is a smiling, happy girl who loves kids, animals, friends, and family.

✦ She exudes confidence in her appearance.

BLAME IT ON RIO

Maya is not afraid to be goofy, nor is she afraid to be sexy. Indeed, Maya is a native of Rio de Janeiro, which means she is Carioca, and the greatest fear of a Carioca is *not* being sexy—because Rio de Janeiro is a wild city between the feral jungle and the deep blue sea and Rio is hot, in more ways than one. Rio is beautiful and sexy and full of life, and the men and women who live there try to reflect that with how they live, how they look.

Maya is not afraid to be pretty, not afraid to be stylish, not afraid to be sexy—and apparently not afraid of death by drowning in frigid water or body-slamming coral reefs in tropical waters.

If you didn't know she was a gutsy big-wave surfer who has nearly died several times from Portugal to Teahupoo, you might think Maya was a fashion model.

She is. But there is more to her than that.

Look on social media and you will also see many images of Maya working hard to stay fit: swimming in pools, working out on treadmills, using weight equipment and balance balls, balancing on one foot doing yoga. She is doing this to maintain her fit appearance, but Maya also works hard to stay strong. For this 5'6", 120-pound, 29-year-old Brazilian girl, the next near-death experience in giant surf is always right around the corner.

And she wants to be prepared—body, mind, and soul.

NEAR DEATH AT NAZARÉ

In October 2013 Maya Gabeira drowned and came as close to dying as a girl can get without actually dying by drowning. The Brazilian was encased in a rubber wet suit and inflatable safety vest, feet strapped into a 6'1" tow board, and was holding onto a tow rope while her Brazilian partner, Carlos Burle, drove a PWC that whipped her into giant waves at Nazaré, Portugal.

Nazaré the surf spot is named for the town in central Portugal, 60 miles north of Lisbon. Nazaré is an excellent place to witness the Atlantic in full roar. High cliffs dramatically overlook a surf spot formed where a 16,000-foot-deep underwater canyon funnels Atlantic Ocean energy from 115 miles out and straight at those 300-foot-high cliffs.

Everything about Nazaré is big: the cliffs, the amount of energy, and the waves that form on the reef. When all that energy comes abruptly from out of the

Maya Gabeira dropping in at Nazaré
Photo courtesy Red Bull

canyons, it roars up and forward into a giant, cold, challenging big wave some say is most likely to produce that elusive 100-foot wave all serious big-wave surfers are hunting for.

On this October day in 2013, Gabeira was towing with Brazilian big-wave surfer Carlos Burle. Two other Brazilians were on the ski and rescue sled with them: Felipe "Gordo" Cesarano on the ski and Pedro "Scooby" Viana on the sled behind Gabeira.

To make a long, harrowing, near-death and rescue story short, Burle towed Gordo into a 50-footer; then, as he was picking up the surfer, he flipped the ski and lost his radio. Scooby wanted the next one, but Gabeira evoked the "lady's first" deal. Scooby backed off. So did Gabeira, as Burle towed into two mackers, but Gabeira wouldn't drop the rope and go. In the channel, Gabeira and Burle had a chat in what had to be passionate Brazilian Portuguese.

Burle reminded Maya she was there to go big, and that is what she did on the next moose of a wave. Gabeira dropped the rope as Burle scooted off to safety, while behind him an avalanche chased Gabeira. Going straight down and fast, Gabeira made it over two big chops, fell on the third, and disappeared under a mountain of whitewater.

"This wave was probably double the size of whatever I had ridden in my life," Gabeira said on the Red Bull documentary about the incident. "Very, very bumpy and very fast. I've never gone that fast on a surfboard before. I broke my ankle on the wave, on the third or the fourth bump, and from there I just went face-first and got pounded by that wave, and then the whole thing started."

> I've never gone that fast on a surfboard before. I broke my ankle on the wave, on the third or the fourth bump, and from there I just went face-first and got pounded by that wave, and then the whole thing started.

THE WHOLE THING

Maya's world went from black to white. Underwater, everything was black, and she thought her time was up. To her surprise, when she made it to the surface she was not in the clouds, listening to angels, but now everything was white. "I couldn't see," Gabeira says on the Red Bull documentary. "I couldn't see and I had no senses, but I could still breathe somehow. But I knew I was in serious trouble, and I knew I had to count on my instincts . . . and on Carlos."

Carlos saw his partner wipe out and caught sight of her as she dealt with the next wave. She held her nose and went under the second wave and disappeared. Carlos lost sight of her. He prowled the space between the exploding whitewater and the shore break, afraid for his partner and scanning the whitewater for the black dot. When he saw her, he came in fast on the ski, but she had little strength left, and the sled hit her on the head.

Burle came in again and tried to grab her with his arm, but missed. In desperation, Maya grabbed onto the tow rope and got water-skied underwater for several seconds. That just about finished her. After that she was drowning, floating facedown in the whitewater, helpless. Lifeless?

Matt Skenazy continued the story on outside.com: "Fifteen feet from shore, she bobs in the churning surf like driftwood. At this point, she's been facedown in the water for more than a minute. Burle ditches the Jet Ski and swims her to shore, where he and a lifeguard give her CPR. Two minutes later, she vomits half a gallon of water and begins to breathe."

On the beach, a dozen bystanders hover and film, while three guys carry her body up the beach and start CPR. Ask any lifesaving professional and they'll tell you that CPR doesn't work a majority of the time. But it worked on Maya. After getting pummeled by several 50-foot waves and half drowned, she came back to life and went straight to the hospital to start a long rehab.

TO TOW, OR NOT TO TOW

In this modern world, when a good-looking Brazilian girl nearly drowns in giant surf—or an Australian pro is assaulted by a white shark in the middle of a contest—the whole world has access to images, almost immediately. The whole world saw Maya Gabeira almost drown at Nazaré, and the incident caused some philosophical unrest in the ranks of big-wave surfers.

On CNN two days after the incident, Laird Hamilton questioned whether Maya should have been out in surf of that size and intensity: "She doesn't have the skill to be in these conditions," Laird said. "She should not be in this kind of surf."

It is well known in surfing circles that Maya's paddle-surfing abilities in small to medium surf are average, but there are many sides to the argument of whether only highly skilled surfers should be towed into giant waves.

In the past the standard has been that a surfer should have proved himself/herself as a paddler in giant waves before being allowed to tow. Maya is not known for paddling into giant waves, and many questioned whether a girl—or anyone—should be towed into 50-foot, freezing-cold waves breaking with Atlantic power in front of high cliffs.

If Maya's basic surfing skills were questioned by some, her training and preparation for big waves was defended by California big-wave surfer Greg Long. "You don't need to be a good small-wave surfer to ride big waves," Long was quoted in that *Outside* magazine article. "There are a lot of big-wave surfers who are average surfers—they're just fearless and have figured out how to ride big waves. She has dedicated her life to managing these risks. Her ability is there."

WHO'S THAT GIRL?

So who is this mad Carioca, apparently not afraid of death by drowning? Gabeira was born in Rio de Janeiro in 1987. Her father, Fernando Gabeira, is a legendary leftist politician and founding member of the Brazilian Green Party. Her mother is Yamê Reis, a successful Brazilian fashion designer.

Getting the picture? Radical leftist and stylish mom = Maya Gabeira getting stylishly radical, going left.

PAPA

Fernando Gabeira was a leftist during a time when Rio de Janeiro was the center of a coup d'état by the Brazilian military—aided by the United States. That inspired Gabeira to go underground, train as a terrorist, and plot against the military government. Working with MR8, a terrorist group trying to install a Socialist government in Brazil, Gabeira was an accessory to the 1969 kidnapping of American Ambassador Charles Elbrick, who was freed in a prisoner exchange and led to the publishing of antigovernment screeds.

The Brazilian secret police hunted Gabeira down with a vengeance. Gabeira exchanged gunfire with the police, and he was injured, captured, and tortured.

During the 1970 World Cup, Gabeira was swapped for the kidnapped Swiss ambassador. He lived in exile in France for many years but was granted amnesty in the 1980s and returned to Brazil, "to begin his career as Brazil's rock and roll politician," according to the *Lost Sambista* blog.

In 1979 Fernando Gabeira published his best-selling memoir *O Que Isto Companheiro?* (*Where Are You, Comrade?*).

Even in libertine Rio de Janeiro, Gabeira was scandalous, admitting he was bisexual while living as a terrorist and appearing on the beach in a very brief, crocheted thong bikini. Even on the beaches of Rio, this was considered shocking. "The photos hit the media and caused a national stir," according to the *Lost Sambista*, "the gay, pot-smoking terrorist, politically active with a liberation and green agenda."

The kidnapping of the American ambassador and Gabeira's memoir were the inspiration for the 1997 movie *Four Days in September*, which was nominated for an Academy Award for Best Foreign Film.

In 2009 Gabeira apologized, saying he would never act against the United States again.

DAAAAAD!

Remember, this is Maya's dear old dad. "He's a very tough man," Gabeira said to Susan Casey in *Women's Health*. "Like, really, really tough." Just like his daughter letting go of the rope and whipping into dangerous bombs at Teahupoo and Nazaré, Fernando Gabeira has always gone for it. A founding member of Brazil's Green Party, he ran for mayor of Rio de Janeiro in 2008 and barely lost. He ran for governor of Rio de Janeiro state in 2010 and also lost.

Gabeira married Yamê Reis in 1982 and they had two daughters, Tami in 1983 and Maya in 1987. Maya's parents divorced in 1999, and that sent Maya spinning off in unpleasant directions.

DIVORCE IS THE ALCHEMY FOR GREAT SURFERS?

Maya is not the first accomplished surfer to flee to the ocean from a broken home: Sixties rebel Miki Dora was the product of a dysfunctional family, women's world champion Layne Beachley was adopted, and Lisa Andersen was a teenage runaway. Legend Kelly Slater also came from a broken home. Jay Moriarity moved to Santa Cruz at 9 years old with his divorced mom and threw himself into the surf at Pleasure Point. All of these surfers came from houses divided around the time they started surfing. They took their heartbreak into the ocean and poured their energies into and found family and community in the surf—drowning their inner sorrow in thrills and endorphins and the beauty of wind and waves.

That is what happened with Maya Gabeira. Her parents divorced when she was 12—an impressionable age. "From 12 to 14 I had a very hard time," Gabeira told Susan Casey for an article in *Women's Health*. "I was very young, and Rio's a big city. You can go in the wrong direction. I was partying too much."

Mom kicked Maya out of the house and she went to live with dad, who wasn't around much and trusted Maya with total freedom. "His trust made her determined to change her ways," Susan Casey wrote. "'I was trying to find something that I'd really like to do,' [Maya said] 'that I'd dedicate myself to, and that would give me some focus in life.'"

According to fashion blogger Carlee Wallace on the Lululemon website, "It was her boyfriend at the time and, she laughingly admits, the movie *Blue Crush* that got her into the water. 'I thought [surfing] was the coolest thing I could do, then I realized it was very hard, and it became cooler because it's hard.'"

Learning to surf is challenging, frustrating, stimulating. It's a lot of paddling and falling, hard work and frustration, getting beat and overcoming failure, getting sand in your ears; and all of these things are what a depressed brain craves and a broken heart needs. Maya craved it, and she threw herself into surfing.

AUSTRALIA TO HAWAII

At 15 years old, Maya moved to Australia on an exchange program for eight months. She lived and surfed with friends on Australia's Gold Coast.

In Australia Maya decided that making a living as a surfer was her career path—a decision that didn't go over too well with her parents back in Rio. They stopped sending her support money to force her to return to Brazil. She came home for a while, but Hawaii was calling to her. "They couldn't understand what I was doing," Maya said to Susan Casey. "The best thing was just not to be nearby so we wouldn't fight so much. And that's how it went for three years. We didn't really talk."

This was all around 2003–2004. Maya was 16, working as a waitress at night, surfing all day, running a lot, trying to find herself. She was lonely, but she was doing what she loved and trying to find a way to make a life of it.

Back then and now, there were and are a lot of random Brazilian girls working in food trucks and as waitresses on the North Shore. According to Maya's sister, Tami, Maya surfed Velzyland often and was inspired to ride big waves by seeing Jamilah Star at Waimea Bay. So how did this particular random Brazilian girl evolve into a big-wave surfer?

BIG DAY AT THE BAY

Maya surfed Sunset Beach on the North Shore as much as she could. It's an addicting wave that requires a great deal of physical effort and is equally punishing and rewarding. Many many men and women over the years have dedicated their lives to surfing Sunset.

She worked her way up at Sunset Beach and then looked to the west. One of Maya's turning points was a big day at Waimea Bay in 2005. This was a giant day, where Maya made the drop on the biggest wave she had ever attempted. "I was high for about ten days afterward," Maya told Susan Casey. "I found my passion out there."

LEARNING TO TOW

In *The Encyclopedia of Surfing*, Matt Warshaw tagged Maya as the "Indestructible goofy footer from Brazil, four-time winner of the Billabong XXL Best Female Performance Awards. . . . Gabeira began tow surfing with fellow Brazilian Carlos Burle in 2006, and the following year she earned the first of four Billabong XXL Best Female Performance Awards."

Maya won the Billabong XXL Best Female Performance Award from 2007 to 2010.
Photo: Lucia Griggi

Maya pulling in at Teahupoo
Photo courtesy Red Bull

TEAHUPOO = BAD ROMANCE

On November 1, 2007, Maya towed into the wrong wave on a big day at Teahupoo. She was well aware of the dangers of Teahupoo, which Laird Hamilton described as being "driven through a cheese grater by a steamroller." Maya was prepared. She had been in Tahiti for six weeks, training on land and riding Teahupoo in its many moods—small and large, windy and clean. She broke eight boards in that six weeks. And then a giant swell approached, bringing two dozen of the world's biggest adrenalin junkies flooding into Papeete.

You can see the wave on YouTube. This is not an über-giant day at Teahupoo, but it's big. Maya lets go of the rope too early, gets stuck in a shelf at the top, air drops over the ledge, wipes out at the bottom, and goes over the falls, stuck in the lip, facedown—kaboom!

Maya in Hawaii, 2009
Photo: Lucia Griggi

It was nasty; there were a lot of guys watching, and chivalry kicked in. Maya was wearing two flotation vests, which helped get her to the surface. She survived, again.

DUNGEONS DRAG IN

In 2009 Maya towed into a moose of a wave at Dungeons, a big-wave reef in South Africa that is the antipodean version of Mavericks: a big, cold right, breaking way out to sea, in waters absolutely infested with white sharks. But where Mavericks breaks in December, Dungeons breaks in August, in the middle of the South African winter.

That wave earned Maya a nomination for Biggest Wave in the 2010 XXL Awards.

CURVES AND COURAGE

From random Brazilian girl working in a North Shore food truck in 2003, by 2009 Gabeira was hitting superstar status—for her courage and her curves—according to *The Encyclopedia of Surfing*:

> Gabeira received an ESPY award in 2009 as the Best Female Action Sports Athlete, and the following year she was named top Female Action Sports Athlete at the Teen Choice Awards. In 2011 the diminutive but buxom Brazilian placed third in *Transworld Surf* magazine's list of the "Top Ten Hottest Girls in Surfing." Determined to move her marker up even further, in 2013 she posed more or less topless in *Sports Illustrated*, and in 2014, and in 2014 was featured (dressed, but barely) in Brazilian *Playboy* and *GQ* Brasil."

CHUMBAWAMBA

If you're searching the jukebox in your head, thinking of the perfect theme song for the life of Maya Gabeira, perhaps Chumbawumba's "Tubthumping" is the one. When she gets knocked down, she gets up again.

In 2011 Maya was part of the crew of big-wave hellmen who tackled Teahupoo for the infamous Code Red swell. Maya towed into a wave and made it, but she kept going past the point in the channel where all the boats and PWC sit in deep water. Past that point, Maya couldn't get out of the wave. She wiped out on the shallowest part of the reef and took five waves on the head over a very shallow, treacherous reef. So shallow, three attempts to rescue her on PWC failed, until Tahitian local Vetea "Poto" David managed to grab the unconscious Gabeira and take her to safety in the channel.

You can see the whole story on the redbull.com website: Maya's bad wipeout in 2011, the underwater apnea and physical training, the trips to Puerto Escondido in Mexico to work on the paddling in and tube-riding, and then her return to Teahupoo in 2013. She gets back on the horse that threw her, pulls into a giant barrel, and kicks out in the channel—safe, sound, and smiley.

RETURN TO NAZARÉ

Go to redbull.com, look through STORIES, and you will also see a video about Maya's return to Nazaré in October 2015. This 5-minute video will introduce you to Garrett McNamara, Nazaré, and Carlos Burle and show how the wave is set up and how the surfers are set up to challenge it.

In the video, Maya talks about getting back on the wave that nearly killed her two years before. In that two years she had gone through back surgeries and both mental and physical rehab. Then in October 2015 she returned with Carlos

Maya tames a tamer beast on her return to Nazaré in October 2015.
Photo courtesy Red Bull

Maya and her Nazaré posse—Pedro Scooby, Felipe Cesarano, and Carlos Burle—prepare to surf at Porto de Abrigo in Nazaré, Portugal, October 27, 2013.
Photos courtesy Red Bull

Maya with her friend, mentor, driver, inspiration, and rescuer Carlos Burle

Maya out at Nazaré, first break of the season 2016
Photo: Lucia Griggi

Burle, took up the rope, and once again did what she loved: towing into mean, green Atlantic bombs in front of those high cliffs.

At the end of the video, Maya describes her mind-set as of October 2015: "You know I never really think about giving up. To me it's like, life gives you challenges and then you have to face them and you have to overcome them and you have to reassure what path you are on. . . . I feel strong now again, after a long time of feeling very fragile."

Maya Gabeira is tough. Like, really really tough.

Keala Kennelly challenging the green monster at Teahupoo
Photo: Tim McKenna

Born: August 13, 1978
Birthplace: Hanalei, Kauai

NOT FEARLESS, BOLD

People are going to love me or hate me, but as long as I am happy and comfortable with myself, that is all that really matters.

—Keala Kennelly

INTRODUCING KEALA

If you're the kind of person who reads the intros to books, then you will already know a little about Keala Kennelly from reading her XXL speech in the intro to *this* book. Going up against some of the best male tuberiders in the world, Keala won the XXL Best Barrel Award for 2015—taking home $10,000 for getting whipped into an evil monster of a barrel at Teahupoo that swallowed her whole and spit her out whole. Go back and read all about it in the intro. She's gnarly. She made a great speech.

But that was so 2015. What has she done recently?

GIRLS JUST WANNA HAVE FUN

Girls just wanna have fun. Keala Kennelly is a girl, and she likes to have fun—but she sometimes has a funny interpretation of fun. Take a look at Keala's life on social media and you will see her swimming and dancing and mugging with and professing her gratitude and devotion to the love of her life: Nikki DiSanto. Keala is happy and gay and not afraid to say both out loud and proud. It seems that she isn't really afraid of anything, physical or emotional—whether it's taking off on bombs at Teahupoo and nearly losing her face or placing public kissy face on Nikki on the red carpet.

Round round get around, Keala gets around. She is also an actress and a DJ who once opened for Snoop Dogg. She's a spirited gal not at all afraid to be herself, stand tall in giant Teahupoo barrels or stand up for herself as a lesbian.

Who is she, and where does all this energy come from?

ROOTS

Keala was born in Hanalei, Kauai, in 1978 to parents who surfed. The Kennelly *ohana* was a house divided when Keala was a teenager. A controversial article in *Surfer* magazine published right after her parents' split portrayed her as angry at her mother and fiercely loyal to her father. But that family has since healed, as has Keala's soul. "The truth is I come from an awesome family. My parents both surf and raised me and my two brothers with a lot of love. We all surfed together as a family when I was growing up, and my parents sacrificed a lot to support my surfing career."

READIN', 'RITIN', 'RITHMETIC, AND READY TO RUMBLE

Keala's first fight was with a boy at Kapaa High School, on the east side of Kauai. If you envision a peaceful, idyllic, one-room schoolhouse where everyone and the teachers surf—that is way wrong. When Laird Hamilton attended Kapaa it was one of the three most violent high schools in the entire United States. And it wasn't much better when Keala attended. She learned the four Rs: readin', 'ritin', 'rithmetic, and ready to rumble. She fought with boys; she fought with "*titas*"— tough local girls often an angry mix of Polynesian, Portuguese, and Asian blood. ". . . and then came that defining moment against the big Samoan transvestite"; Matt George wrote. "Keala never lost a fight. Maintaining a 3.5 GPA through the mayhem also meant she could surf as much as she liked."

She liked to surf much, and that's a good thing on Kauai, because there is much surf. Keala was born the same year as Andy Irons. Bruce Irons was born a year later. They all grew up surfing the North Shore of Kauai, and Keala was the tomboy trying to keep up with two of the best surfers that island ever produced. "Well, it was a slow progression," Keala told Laia Garcia on lennyletter.com. "I grew up with Andy and Bruce, and it was like the whole tomboy thing trying to tag along with the boys, you know? I just wanted those guys to respect me. It's like a bravado, macho thing if you could ride through big waves, and they were always pushing each other to ride those kinds of waves, so I just followed their lead."

IDENTITY

While Keala tussled with the challenging surf of Kauai, she also struggled with her sexual identity. "I knew I liked girls from a very young age," Keala said to Garcia. "But I also knew that my liking girls wasn't cool or accepted, so I tried really hard to be straight, and I could tell that it was not my thing! It was really scary."

Growing up on Kauai, Keala dealt with the surf and dealt with herself, but through a combination of her competitive nature, and the nurture of her family and friends and fellow Kauai surfers, it came together. She did well in local contests on Kauai and around the Hawaiian Islands—surfing in the Girl's Division of course. At the United States Surfing Championships in 1992, Keala placed third, then second in 1993, then fourth in 1994. At the 1994 ISA World Surfing Championships in Rio de Janeiro, Brazil, Keala finished third in the Open Women's division.

GOING PRO

Keala turned pro in 1995 at age 17 and began traveling on the World Qualifying Series—the farm league for the World Championship Tour. In 1997 she finished second on the WQS, and that flowed her onto the WCT in 1998. At the Gotcha Black Pearl Women's Pro at Teahupoo, Tahiti, Keala won her first event and began to establish her dangerous, death or glory dominance at the dangerous Tahitian reef. According to Matt Warshaw in *The Encyclopedia of Surfing*:

Kennelly's blunt, hard-charging style wasn't a natural fit within the regulated confines of the world pro tour, but she nonetheless became one of the circuit's most compelling figures, launching airs where other women kicked out, and riding deep inside the tube at places like Pipeline and Teahupoo. She won her first major world tour event at Teahupoo; the following year she won the Op Pro/Mentawais specialty event, and in 2002 she again won at Teahupoo.

Keala peaked as a pro in 2003. She started the season at #1 in the rankings, won the Billabong Pro Teahupoo event for the third time, and also won the Roxy Pro in Fiji and the Turtle Bay Pro on the North Shore of Oahu, Hawaii.

At the end of 2003, Keala ended up #2 in the world, finishing runner-up to multi-world champion Layne Beachley.

TRANSITIONS

Two thousand and three was her best year as a pro. Keala stayed in the Top 10 through 2007, but she began a transition into acting, and then took an alternative route that other male surfers have taken: that of the noncompeting free surfer, thrill seeker, extremist. The professional free surfer. The big-wave charger.

Keala grew up on Kauai and went to the same high school as Laird Hamilton, who was one of the godfathers of tow surfing.

In 2005 she was the first woman to tow surf Teahupoo. Keala's pioneering session was covered by the ASP World Tour website. "I've been thinking about it for weeks now and talking myself into it, but you get scared thinking you are going to fall and if you make a mistake it's going to cost you your life."

Known as the Queen of Chopes, Kennelly ended up winning the Billabong Pro Teahupoo three times, in 2000, 2002, and 2003 at the left-hander, and she showed little fear. "I let go of the rope, saw it throwing, and just did what I normally do when I surf out here and pulled in and started pumping really hard."

She went on to say, "The wave itself is such a marvel; it's so treacherous and yet so beautiful at the same time. It has so much energy, I just sort of feed off it. When I am out there, I have so much adrenaline running through my veins, it drives me—I love it. I live for that feeling. Basically I just throw myself over the ledge and pray I don't stack it on the drop. The reward is definitely worth the risk."

TOWING JAWS

In 2009 Keala towed Jaws for the first time. "Towing Jaws is so different than towing in at Teahupoo," she wrote on surfermag.com.

At Teahupoo you know you are on a BIG wave because it is throwing down the line in front of you and you are just trying to hold your line in the barrel and come out. At Jaws, the big wave is behind you, so the first few waves I thought they were really small, it wasn't until I looked behind me on the third wave I caught that I saw this big meat-grinder running up behind me.

The feeling when you let go of the rope is so strange. When you are gliding along, it feels like you are snowboarding down a liquid slope. On most of my waves I just negotiated chops as I ran for the shoulder. I was not trying to do big fade turns and risk getting gobbled up on my first session at Jaws on a borrowed board. I caught about seven or eight waves before my legs completely gave out from exhaustion.

Keala paddling into Jaws
Photo: Erik Aeder

Keala paddling into Jaws
Photo: Erik Aeder

NELSCOTT CHAMPION: 2010

In November 2010—a few days after the death of her friend Andy Irons—Keala won the Nelscott Big Wave Event in Oregon. She talked about the state of big wave events for women with surfermag.com:

> The Big Wave World Tour is fairly new and with anything that is new it takes a while for things to catch on. When I started competing, there wasn't even a girls division in my local contests—I had to compete against the boys. Then we finally were able to scrape together a six-person girls heat. Now there are too many girls entering events and you have to put some of them on the alternate list. So it just takes a few women showing up and getting it started. That is the main reason why I came to this event

in Oregon—to help give the women that extra push towards getting more big-wave events for women in the future.

She went on to address whether there are enough top-level women to hold big-wave contests, saying that there are many surfers who aren't well known simply because they don't have sponsorship—"women like Paige Alms and Andrea Moller, who are out at Jaws every massive swell and have never even been nominated for a Billabong XXL award. I think if there were more big-wave events for women in the future, that would give more women the opportunity to get sponsored and also give them something to aspire to."

FACE-OFF

Entering the second decade of the twenty-first century, Keala Kennelly was determined to become the face of women's big-wave surfing and raise the profile of what women could do in big and dangerous surf. And in doing so, she almost lost her own face.

Big wave legend Greg Noll is fond of saying, "It's never the one you think it's gonna be, kid." Which means the wipeouts you think are going to drown and/or kill you usually don't, and it's often the little, benign wipeouts that do the most damage.

That was certainly true for Keala. She flew to Teahupoo in September 2011 to meet a giant swell that produced the Code Red session—arguably the heaviest, most dangerous day at Teahupoo up to that point.

Keala took the Code Red rope and did okay, as she remembered to Joe Turpel on surfermag.com:

. . . there was one barrel that I was really pleased with. I was pretty deep and the barrel started bending so hard on the reef. I started to feel the front of my board lifting up (from the lip exploding white-wash up into the barrel). I got heavy on my back foot and started rolling up the windows on the car as if I was going to fall backward into the barrel. So I shifted all my weight back onto my front foot, held my line, and got spit out of the barrel. I was really stoked (and relieved) to make it out of that one.

So Keala survived the Code Red day and moved up several notches on the Gnarlometer. Three days later the swell had dropped enough to hold the Billabong Pro. Keala was invited to surf in a special expression session in honor of Andy Irons. "I felt really honored that Bruce invited me to come surf with him to honor Andy," Keala told Joe Turpel.

Those boys are like brothers to me, and I love them so much. The vibe in the water was kind of heavy, you know. Bruce was feeling the loss of his brother big time, and he had all eyes on him. It must be so hard to be mourning in the public eye like that. I really felt for him in that moment. I hate to see someone I care about so much suffering like that.

OUCH

And then Keala did some suffering of her own. The wave that got her wasn't much by Teahupoo standards, but you remember what Greg Noll said. . . . "It was a pretty regular-looking wave," Keala said to Joe Turpel.

I took off and it kind of had a bit of bump that kept me from pulling into the barrel straight away. I had to make some adjustments and then saw that the next section was going to barrel, so I bottom-turned and parked it in the barrel. I traveled for a bit, had to negotiate the foam-ball, and that may have thrown me off and made me have to draw a higher line. I thought I was coming out, but the lip just caught me in the head and threw me straight into the reef before I even realized what happened.

The pain was intense and I knew I was hurt. I could see lots of blood, but I had no idea it was as bad as it was.

ALMOST THE END OF THE ROAD

Teahupoo is also known as End of the Road, which means it's not really close to anything, tucked away on the southeast side of Tahiti Iti. The next couple of hours couldn't have been fun, as Keala was picked up efficiently by the Water Patrol and taken to shore on a PWC. There was a medical tent for the Billabong Pro, but they knew she needed serious care, so she was in the ambulance 20 minutes later for a quick ride to Taravao Hospital, about 10 miles away on the isthmus that connects the larger Tahiti Nui with the smaller Tahiti Iti.

Doctors at Taravao knew it was serious; they sent her off to the main hospital in Papeete, another 90-minute ambulance ride away.

At the main hospital in Papeete, Keala struck a pose for some pre-op photos that Matt Warshaw described wryly: "When a 2011 Teahupoo wipeout flayed opened the right side of her face, she arched an eyebrow and posed for some pre-medical-treatment photos that turned the stomachs of even the gnarliest male big-wave hellmen."

When Keala was done taking ghastly selfies, doctors performed a CT scan to be sure she hadn't broken her skull or cheek or injured her neck. The CT scan came back okay, and then she went into surgery, where they removed pieces of reef from her face and gave her fifty-one external stitches and more internal stitches to repair the damage to her eye, head, chin, and jaw.

BLUE CRUSH

In 2002 Keala Kennelly began her acting career with a role in *Blue Crush*. The story is about Mary Anne Chadwick (played by Kate Bosworth), a talented woman surfer who has Pipeline issues. Mary Anne smacked her head on the reef at Pipeline once, and that put the fear into her—a fear she has to overcome to challenge Pipeline and thrive as a pro.

In the movie *Blue Crush*, Keala Kennelly plays herself, an experienced, tough local girl who is comfortable at Pipe. For the finale of the movie, Chadwick and Keala meet in a heat at serious Pipe. Chadwick keeps pulling back from waves while Keala is charging, and possibly the best bit of acting in the whole movie happens when Keala paddles up to Chadwick and cajoles her into facing her fears: "What are you *doin'*?"

Keala yells at Chadwick to go! Paddle! Anne Marie paddles into a wave and doesn't hold back, and she still wipes out, hits the bottom, and has all her fears come true. But then she shake, shake, shakes it off, paddles back out, catches a bomb, pulls into a giant barrel backside, and gets spit out the end. (See the Rochelle Ballard profile for how that stunt was staged.)

Keala charging at Jaws
Photo: Erik Aeder

RETURN TO TEAHUPOO

The fiction of *Blue Crush* prophesied Keala Kennelly's reality. Teahupoo severely damaged and scarred half of Keala's face, and if she never returned to the spot or uttered the word "Tahiti," again, no one would have blamed her.

But you can't keep a tough woman down, and she did return to Teahupoo.

Keala got whipped into a giant hole, got gobbled up by the dragon, wiped out spectacularly, lived to tell about it, and a few months later took the stage at the 2015 WSL XXL Big Wave Awards to accept a $10,000 check and make a whopper of an acceptance speech. (Read the intro if you bypassed it.)

NOT FEARLESS, BRAVE

The media likes to refer to Keala as "fearless," but that is incorrect, as she explained to Laia Garcia at lennyletter.com:

> First of all, I'm not fearless at all! That's such a huge misconception. I feel like to be fearless, you have to be completely ignorant of the fact that what you're doing is dangerous and can cause you bodily harm. And I'm super-aware that all those things can happen, so I think that's more being brave and not fearless. Fear is healthy because it keeps you alive! Fearlessness makes you do stupid things.

QUEEN BEE

So that is how the queen bee of women's gnarly surfing earned her crown: nurtured by Kauai, and the Irons Brothers and a lot of helping hands from Kauai to Maui to Tahiti to Mavericks—including her squeeze, Nikki DiSanto. Keala Kennelly is extremely determined to face her fears and live up to her own expectations, even at the risk of severe injury and/or death.

Good times/bad times, Keala has seen more than her share in her time. She has suffered brutal lickings at Teahupoo and Jaws and elsewhere, but she has also earned the respect of the surfing and civilian world.

If the eighth deadly sin is living an unchallenged, not interesting life, Keala is not a sinner.

> ### Fear is healthy because it keeps you alive! Fearlessness makes you do stupid things.

Andrea taking a sideways drop,
dealing with that Maui wind at
Pe'ahi/Jaws
Photo: Erik Aeder

Born: September 16, 1979
Birthplace: São Paulo, Brazil

WATERWOMAN

WATERMEN AND WATERWOMEN

The Encyclopedia of Surfing defines "waterman" as:

> A surfer who is comfortable in a wide variety of ocean conditions, has a broad store of oceanic knowledge, and is accomplished in a range of surfing-related activities, including diving, swimming, sailing, bodysurfing, fishing, spearfishing, surf canoeing, and oceangoing rescue work. Most watermen are from Hawaii. Surf journalist Dave Parmenter in 2000 described Makaha resident Brian Keaulana as "without a doubt the greatest all-around waterman alive, [someone who can] ride a shortboard or longboard at a world-class level, steer a four-man Hawaiian canoe through the Makaha bowl at 12 feet, and tow-surf the local cloud break—all in a single afternoon."

Matt Warshaw names Pat Curren, Laird Hamilton, Dave Kalama, and Mark Healey as examples of talented watermen. If you're looking for a definition of "waterwoman," go to the island of Maui and get in a car accident or do something stupid. The paramedic who comes to your rescue might be Andrea Moller—a Brazilian woman who pretty much defines the parameters of the thoroughly modern waterwoman.

Andrea Moller isn't included in *The Encyclopedia of Surfing*, but if she were, the words would look something like this:

Originally from a small island in Brazil, Andrea Moller moved to Maui in 1998 to compete as a windsurfer. In the almost twenty years since, she has established herself as a top outrigger canoe paddler and competitor, a stand up paddler and competitor, and one of the top female big-wave surfers in the world, whether paddling or towing into waves from Jaws to Mavericks. Moller was the first woman to paddle and tow at Pe'ahi/Jaws. In 2014 Moller was nominated for the Women's Performance of the Year Award at the Billabong XXL Big Wave Awards—the wave that attracted the most attention was a beast at Jaws. In 2016 Moller won the Women's Performance Award at the World Surf League XXL Awards and delivered a hard-earned and heartfelt acceptance speech [see below].

Moller is pushing the limits of what is possible for women in giant surf, and she has worked hard to become one of the best all-around ocean waterwomen on Maui and in the world, from racing OC1 to charging giant waves.

How did she get there?

ROOTS

Andrea Moller grew up in Brazil, with water all around her, and in her blood. Her parents owned a marina on the island of Ilhabela, about 80 miles from São Paulo and a short hop from the mainland. Moller grew up learning to have fun with what the terrain and weather conditions offered. The island was safe to explore, and as a young teenager she would swim miles across the channel, windsurf for hours, climb high mountains, bike steep hills—anything grown-ups perceived as difficult or impossible. She considers her childhood one of the greatest influences on her personality.

Andrea left behind her idyllic childhood and beloved island at 17 when she moved to San Diego as an exchange student—while still being close to the ocean. "I refused to move to a big city—like São Paulo—because I knew I would be unhappy far away from the ocean. Since I didn't really know what college I wanted to attend in Brazil, my parents sent me for a four-month English course in San Diego as an exchange student."

Brazilians love Brazil, but Brazilians also have a thing for Hawaii—tropical, warm water, endless wind and wave energy. Of all the Hawaiian islands, windy

Maui is the mecca for sailboarders, and Moller moved to Maui in 1998 to hone her skills and compete as a sailboarder. She liked it and is still there. "From San Diego to Hawaii—initially to visit, and because of windsurfing. When I arrived on Maui and saw the extreme weather conditions—strong winds, big waves, massive waterfalls—I knew I wanted this lifestyle." She registered for college for one semester that turned into "two full college courses, a family, a solid job, and a lot of time in the water." While sailboarding was her initial pursuit, outrigger canoe paddling became the sport that kept her, as well as the friends that became her family.

To support herself, and maybe learn some self-preservation skills, Moller underwent EMT training, graduating in 2008. After working as an EMT for two years, she trained as a paramedic and became licensed in 2011. Today she works full-time as an ambulance paramedic on the North Shore of Maui: Paia, Makawao, Pukalani, Haiku, all the way to Kaumahina—halfway to Hana.

Maui is the place for the water-crazed because there is always wind, the ocean is always moving, and, whether the surf is flat or huge, there is always an excuse to get in the water.

Moller was married to Yves, but the marriage didn't last. "The father of my kid, we were married and ended up eventually getting divorced," Moller told Anna Dimond in an interview for the World Surf League. "I look back and wonder, maybe we got divorced because I really didn't stay at home and be the perfect wife that stays home all day. I was the hardworking [one], going and working full-time and managing the kid and being an athlete. And maybe that could have killed it."

Moller had her daughter, Keala, in 2001 when she was 22 and busy with many things: working as a paramedic, outrigger canoe paddling, stand up paddling. Anna Dimond asked Moller: "Were you nervous that having a baby would derail your athletic dreams?"

I focused more on becoming a professional athlete after I had her. Because before I had my kid, [I had] a lot of time on [my] hands. Once I got pregnant—I was 22, had Keala at 23—so nine months of pregnancy made me think, "I can't wait!" You have your kid, you get back in shape as soon as she's 1 and going to day care or she's easier to drop off with someone for an hour. I was so dying to [surf] again that the 1 hour that I had I would train as hard and as focused as I could. My kid taught me how to manage my time well.

IF LAIRD CAN DO IT . . .

In 2004 Moller moved into two new things: tow surfing and stand up paddling. Both of these water pursuits were innovated in part by Laird Hamilton, and Moller teamed up with Maria Souza, a Brazilian woman who had been married to Laird Hamilton in the 1990s.

Their philosophy: *"If Laird can do it, so can we."*

A bold statement, but Moller and Souza backed up their philosophy with action.

"I was 23 or 24, and my daughter was 1 year old," Moller described her first tow session to Matt Chebatoris on supexaminer.com:

> "The surf was too big and everywhere was closing out, and I didn't have enough time to drive to the other side of the island to catch the wrap-around. So I wanted to just get on the Jet Ski and go tow-in and do fun stuff for 2 hours and then come back to my kid."
>
> The time was around 2004–2005. Andrea partnered with her good friend Maria Souza, Laird Hamilton's ex-wife, and began training in earnest to become a big-wave surfer. They each felt that if Laird could do it, then they could too, but they were always met head on by the glass ceiling of the gender barrier in extreme sports. Not long after, Andrea became the first woman to successfully paddle in at Maui's infamous big wave known simply as Jaws.

Moller explained her attraction to Jaws—and big waves in general—to Anna Dimond in an interview on the World Surf League website:

> There is something about that volume of water; you really have to work with nature. Jaws is just so much stronger than you. Because there's that feeling of risking your life, when you make it, there's a real [sense of] survival. You want the challenge. Each wave you surf out there—every time you're like, "Wow, that was intense." Whereas for regular surfing, for me, I'm constantly trying to do a move and prove [myself]. And in big-wave surfing, it's much more than that. It's not about a turn, or an aerial, it's about surviving. Every time you survive a wave, you want to push it a little more, and a little more.

Moller and Souza wanted to be taken seriously and didn't want to be the women who had to be rescued by the guys. Andrea used tip money from teaching diving to buy a used Jet Ski, and they put in the water hours: "It took us a year," Moller told Dimond. "We trained on the outer reefs, even paddling in too. We wanted to rescue perfectly because when we went to Jaws, if I was the girl who showed up at Jaws and I immediately lost my board and hit the rocks or had to be helped by the guys, I could hear it already like, 'What are they doing there?'"

For Moller—as for a lot of sailboarders/surfers/tow surfers—her sailboarding experience served her well as a tow surfer because sailboarders have the speed to catch waves from behind. Moller learned how to judge which giant lump of water was "*Go!*" or "*Nooooo!*"

Because I was a windsurfer, I learned how to read the wave from behind, like you sail into a wave. Which is very much how tow surfing is: The Jet Ski comes from behind and the wave is forming with you, and you read your waves differently than when you're sitting watching the face of the wave. So it was like second nature. And then of course I knew how to surf, so paddle-in surfing was the next step.

FIRST TOW DAY

Their first tow day was a little fluky, but all was well that ended well, Moller remembered to Anna Dimond:

There's this amazing, glassy beautiful wave on the outer reefs, and we surfed it so much that day. And then our ski started [stalling out]. We thought we better stop here, because if we lose the ski, we'd have to swim a long way home. Which we had done before, so over the years we learned how to fix the ski and we were our own little mechanics. But that day we decided to zoom over to Jaws and just sit in the channel and watch, because we couldn't really tow in with our half-broken Jet Ski.

And I remember we got to the lineup and Maria and I were like, "I think I can do that." We watched for a while, and it was either Yuri [Soledade] or another surfer who said, "Want me to put you in a wave?" There's only a few guys that would ever put a girl on the wave, so we started surfing

Andrea taking the drop
Photo: Erik Aeder

and making it, and from that day on we said, let's go. Once that door opened for us, we were going there every time it was breaking.

CROSS TRAINING INTO SUP

Living on Maui is all about cross-training—by land and sea. Stand up paddling (SUP) when the waves are flat keeps your legs and upper body ready for when the waves are huge. Maui was one of the laboratories for stand up paddling beginning with Laird Hamilton, Dave Kalama, Loch Eggers, and a growing handful of others beginning in the late 1990s and then expanding into the twenty-first century—as other Maui waterpeople stopped wondering what the heck Laird and they were doing and tried it for themselves.

Moller started stand up paddling around 2004 on Maria Souza's tandem surfboard, and immediately set her sights on doing something no woman had done before: Cross the treacherous Kai'wi Channel—aka The Channel of Bones—during the annual Molokai to Oahu paddleboard race.

Paddling a purpose-built 13-footer—which was considered huge for that time—Andrea and Maria left their mark in the history books as the first women's relay to ever cross the channel on a stand up paddleboard. Later, as the equipment began to progress, Andrea successfully crossed the channel as a solo stand up paddler, winning the women's solo race from Molokai to Oahu with back-to-back victories in 2010 and 2011.

TEAM BRADLEY: 2007

In 2007 Andrea joined Team Bradley, a six-woman outrigger canoe team named for canoe maker Sonny Bradley. The team placed first in the Na Wahine O Ke Kai, a grueling outrigger race from Molokai to Oahu.

That year, racing SUP, Andrea placed first in the Quiksilver Edition Paddleboard Relay, a 32-mile race from Molokai across the Oahu Channel. She also took first in the Naish International P. Race.

In 2009 and 2010 Andrea competed in both OC6 [six-person outrigger canoe] and SUP, racking up a lot of victories and most likely flooding her shelves with trophies.

2014 XXL RIDE OF THE YEAR

The beauties continued as every year Moller and Souza refined their tow act: better boards, better driving, better conditioning, more experience. Go online and check out Andrea's 2014 Ride of the Year entry for the XXL Big Wave Awards. Moller gets whipped into a gray, glassy moose of a wave and shows a great deal of muscle and nerve as she flies across the face, nearly gets barreled a couple of times, and kicks out at the end.

That had to be a rush.

She didn't win Ride of the Year, but that one wave raised the esteem of women's big wave surfing in the eyes of the world.

2016: GOOD TIMES, BAD TIMES

The year 2016 was good times and bad times for Andrea Moller—but that's how it goes for extreme athletes. On January 28 Jaws/Pe'ahi was giant. Moller was ready at sunrise, and Brazilian Yuri Soledade was her driver. They launched at Maliko Gulch and were out in the heaving lineup at Jaws before the sun's rays were on the water.

Towed by Soledade, Moller caught some bombs on a big, windy day, and a lot of surfers on the cliff and in the water took notes and took notice.

A few weeks later, on February 11, Moller was back at Jaws on a big day. But this time Moller wiped out and was badly injured—her hamstring pulling away from her bone. She flew to Santa Monica for surgery and was still recuperating when she flew to Orange County in April 2016 to attend the WSL XXL Big Wave Awards.

For the Women's Performance Award, Moller was up against Keala Kennelly, Paige Alms, Emi Erickson, and Bethany Hamilton. That's a tough crowd, but the judges liked the cut of Andrea's jib, and she was awarded $10,000 for putting in the best performance by a female in big waves.

Still nursing that February injury, Moller looked dashing on the red carpet in a little black dress—accessorized by a Brazilian flag. An interviewer asked Moller what the highlights of her year were. She answered: "Well I had a couple of good waves at Pe'ahi, and that's where I live, and I had a ton of fun, and another thing that made me feel in the zone was traveling. Going to Mavericks, to Oahu, and just surfing some other spots. But overall I had fun."

There is something about that volume of water; you really have to work with nature. Jaws is just so much stronger than you. Because there's that feeling of risking your life, when you make it, there's a real [sense of] survival. You want the challenge. Each wave you surf out there—every time you're like, "Wow, that was intense."

Andrea flying at Jaws during winter 2015-2016, but maybe not fast enough. She got drilled, but shook it off and got some more.
Photo: Erik Aeder

Moller accepted the oversize check for $10,000 and made a nice speech in her Brazilian-accented English:

This award means a lot to me. This was the greatest winter, so to win the Women's Performance of the Year and catch some of the biggest waves ever is an honor. I almost feel like I have waited ten years to be here. I even changed my priorities as I went to school and became a paramedic. When I came back to surfing, it was not to win an award; it was for pure fun. This winter was definitely all about fun, and was also a season that pushed me to a new level.

PROFESSIONAL RESCUER, PROFESSIONAL RISK TAKER

There's an irony bubbling around this iron woman. Here's a professional rescuer who spends a lot of her personal time putting her own self in dangerous situations. Her work as a paramedic can be risky too. She works with police and firefighters who mainly handle rescues. When she arrives first on the scene, she does face a greater chance of being attacked or injured, but she accepts that as part of the job: "I . . . actually like the adrenaline while working."

Andrea admits it can be unsettling to see the consequences of extreme activities at work—surfing injuries, drownings, shark attacks, fatal bike accidents—and then go do those crazy things herself. She tries not to think about it while she's surfing or biking, but it does cross her mind. "I try to transform my bad trauma cases from work into a learning experience and preparation for the worst in my personal life. My child is probably the one that suffers the most from what I see at work; she's not allowed to try anything without a helmet—ha-ha, poor kid."

When asked about the strangest thing she has seen on the job, Andrea responded, "It is hard for me to single out one particular call. . . . Happy calls are the healthy baby deliveries. Strange calls are the hanging suicides. Sad calls are the irreversible strokes, heart attacks, and pediatric cases. Fun calls are those where we truly save someone's life."

She finds gratification in helping people, which keeps her going. "It makes me love my job."

Andrea has also used her paramedic experience to save herself and others when she is off duty. With friends she has tended mostly minor injuries like a cut from a surfboard fin or broken bones. Her most serious cases outside of work were not from people she knew personally. She makes sure she's prepared to come to the rescue. "I'm always carrying a first-aid case and an AED [automated external defibrillator] in my car—hoping to be ready for an emergency but not needing to use it on any of my friends."

MAUI NO KA OI

Take a look at Andrea Moller's life on social media and you will see a healthy, happy, and healing mom raising a healthy and happy daughter. You'll see images of Andrea working hard and playing hard. Big waves and big paddleboards. A lot of outdoor activity, blue skies, warm water. Andrea has been on Maui almost twenty years; she has a lot of sweat equity in her life there.

She's done a lot since leaving Ilhabela, but she's only 37 during a time when training and discipline have extended athletic peak performance well into the 40s and beyond.

What's next for Andrea Moller? Her goals are simple: "Live life to the fullest, and give positive motivation to others." Right now she's living life one day at a time, healing from her leg injury and enjoying the fact that she can work again and pay the bills. She wants to be back exploring the giant waters soon, surfing and paddling in exotic places. "There are so many things I haven't done yet."

So there it is: Eat Pray Surf. Andrea Moller left home at age 17 to learn English and found her heart and soul in the wild elements of the Hawaiian Islands. She has dedicated a third of her life to rescuing others, a third to risking her life, and the other third to raising her daughter, who loves sports like her mom. "She's the type of girl that is always stoked to be active, but not stuck on one sport only yet. . . . I'll let her steer her own boat and find her own passion."

The two go surfing, take jiu-jitsu classes, and paddle downwind runs on their two-man canoe together—sorry, two-waterwoman. "There's nothing more important in my life than my daughter—my unconditional love."

Born: July 11, 1986
Birthplace: Newport Beach, California

SOUL SALVATION

GAME CHANGER

While we were assembling the profiles for this book, a lot of people suggested who should be included. Jianca Lazarus is a South African photographer who spends a lot of time on the North Shore of Oahu, when she isn't traveling around the world.

In March 2016 Jianca texted: "I still think you should put Leah Dawson in the book. She is a huge part in women's surfing and changing the face of the way women are looked at in the surf industry. She's a game changer."

Bold statements, but to support them Jianca sent a link to a 3:54 edit of Leah surfing. Leah Dawson is both thoroughly modern and retro, riding a variety of boards—traditional longboards, 70s single fins, modern hulls, skegless—and she's making it look pretty danged good (maybe a little too much soul arching, but whatever). The first shot is of Leah hanging ten in slow motion at what looks like Malibu. Poise and posture, grace and speed. And then there she is arching long bottom turns, pulling into barrels, carving grab-rail cutbacks, and even riding bully style—feet parallel—which goes back to the Hawaiian beach boys of the 1920s.

She clearly is a student and lover of all kinds of surfing.

Clearly this is a woman who loves surfing, loves the ocean, loves what it does to her body and soul. If you had to classify Leah, she would not be a big-wave charger like Keala or Maya, not a pro competitor like Sally or Bethany.

She is all these things: She likes big waves, she competes, she is healthy and lovely; but if you had to classify her as any one thing, that would be "soul surfer."

**Leah Dawson, color-coordinated,
camouflaged, and ready to surf**
Photo: Shannon Marie Quirk

SOUL SURFING

The Encyclopedia of Surfing defines "soul surfer" thusly: "Durable if over-used phrase generally used to describe the type of riding practiced by a non-commercial, non-competitive surfer; a 'pure' surfer; a surfer who rides for personal enrichment only."

Leah Dawson might charge big waves, she might compete from time to time, and she has stood as a model, but in essence she is a "soul surfer": someone who goes surfing purely for the joy of it—for the athletic and aesthetic challenge; for the exercise; for the contact with the elements; for the speed and thrill of riding waves; for the travel and the camaraderie, for the endless equation of different boards on different waves on different days in different countries around the world.

Surfing is an endless, ever-changing equation with many variables, including swell size, swell direction, swell wavelength, wind speed, wind direction, time of day, clouds, sunrise/sunset, tide, bottom contour, crowd, personal mood, personal fitness, and the myriad surfboards available to modern surfers: shortboards, single fins, thrusters, quads, modern longboards, original longboards, skegless, hulls, fish, and combinations of all of these.

Surfing is an ever-changing equation with one product: Surfing = fun.

Leah Dawson appears to be hooked on that equation.

That's the game.

SOULFUL "OSOPHY"

Soul surfers have a tendency to be philosophers, either spoken or written. Soul surfers love to expound on the physical, spiritual, and metaphysical joys of surfing. Watch that 3:54 edit and piece together Leah's narration; you will hear a soul surfer holding forth and get a big slice of this woman's philosophy. She said, "My biggest compliment is not that I surf like a man, but that I surf like a woman. If someone watches me ride a wave, I want them, at the end of it, to know I am in love with the ocean."

That soulful surfing is expounded as she recounts how surfing is about harmony: "I think surfing awakens you more to the way that humans are a part of our natural environment. We have to become in harmony with the ocean in order to ride its waves." And it's more than just competition. "It makes my heart sing when

I see other women out in the water and just playing and rejoicing. They're not out doing tricks and they're not trying to become #1 in the world—they're just going out for their daily medicine."

Ultimately, it's about change:

So when more and more women start feeling beautiful from the inside out—when we wear equipment that makes us feel beautiful, but also doesn't make us sell our sex. When we take our power back and tell the story from our own female voice, that's very spiritual and very connected. Then we're going to recognize that women's surfing may be the biggest growth available in the surf market. It's a massively untapped market that doesn't need to be tapped of its money, it needs to be tapped for its soul. It needs to be brought together to encourage the whole surfing community to make more change together.

ROOTS

Leah is not an Aquarius, but everything else about her nature and nurture is all about water. Her parents are both from Southern California, where they were dedicated surfers and water-skiers. Leah was born in 1986 and has an older brother and younger sister, "who was a prima ballerina for many years. I grew up watching her perform leading roles in classical ballets, which undoubtedly influences what I do on my board."

Born in California, Leah lived in Orlando, Florida, from ages 3 to 18. Her family moved to Florida in 1989 for her dad to produce *The Mickey Mouse Club*. An independent producer, he produced the original live-action *Teenage Mutant Ninja Turtles* films with East Coast surf legend Gary Propper.

Orlando is in the middle of Florida, but it's also the land of lakes. Leah's dad put her on a boogie board behind the family boat, and she stood up first thing.

The next weekend they went surfing, and Leah rode on the front of his board at 7 years old. "After that I was hooked, so on the weekends we would drive from Orlando to play in the ocean."

Leah also grew up in the vicinity of Kelly Slater. Her family bought a beach house near Sebastian Inlet when Leah was 7. "We went to the beach and played in the water every waking hour."

Growing up, Leah played nearly every sport you can think of—jump rope, diving, soccer, basketball, golf, softball, swimming, and water polo—but for her nothing compared with being at the beach. The other activities "fueled my athleticism," she said, "but didn't come close to the spiritual connection I felt to surfing."

Once her family had the beach house, she surfed nearly every weekend and all through the summers. When she was 12 her parents let her go to Cabo San Lucas with her friend Kira Sheppard and her family. "I was hooked on surf travel immediately, and did so every summer thereafter."

Leah had met Kira at her first ESA event when she was 7. As a high school student, Leah competed in longboard and shortboard amateur events. A few years in a row she won the NSSA Scholastic Surfer of the Year Award. She was just about the only kid who lived far from the beach, which made it easy for her to focus on her studies.

Leah graduated from her Orlando high school in the Top 10. She applied to Pepperdine, Point Loma, and the University of Hawaii. "I knew I wanted to go to school right by the beach," Leah said.

Her brother was in the US Navy stationed at Pearl Harbor, which made her plea to her parents to go to Hawaii a bit easier. Once she was there, she "fell in love with all that is Hawaii: the nature, the culture, and the amazing waves."

COMPETITION DAYS

After high school Leah focused more on competing in longboard events than shortboard. She traveled to the World Longboard events and was in the Top 10 for eight years. "I always felt I did my best when the waves were good, especially good size. I've always been attracted to powerful surf."

Her best performance on the longboarding stage was third in the world. Other competitive highlights include winning the Women's Pipeline Pro longboard event and getting second in the shortboard event.

In an expression session event at the Deus 9ft and Single in Bali, she won the women's event twice and came in third in the single fin shortboard event against all the boys. These formats—45- to 60-minute, six-person heats—were the most fun for Leah because they allowed for camaraderie, rotation, and time to develop rhythm in the ocean.

She also won a couple club contests at Malibu: "Perfect waves always excited me to perform at my best and allow intuition to create my movement."

In her mid-20s, Leah began to lose her interest in competition. For a while competition was fulfilling to her; it allowed her to travel with friends with similar goals and develop an extended family around the world. But when the competition started getting in the way of friendships, her desire to compete diminished. "I realized I no longer wanted to pursue having the thing I love to do most be judged, compared, and trying to be better than anyone but myself."

At 23 she found herself riding a single fin log for the first time and stopped riding high-performance longboards that earned the top scores. Even though her judges' scores weren't improving, Leah felt her surfing was. She was hooked. "I was finally learning what style meant and felt like to me and became unconcerned with doing maneuvers, just drawing lines. I've been mainly riding single fins of all sizes ever since."

In 2012 Leah competed in the World Longboard Championships in China. The Chinese government paid for the event entirely, putting the athletes up in luxurious five-star hotels. Leah felt uncomfortable with such treatment "while there were starving people all around us. I felt a bit like a puppet, for promotional use to encourage surf travel to China." She left knowing that surfing meant more to her than competition and industry. "My soul was wanting something deeper through surfing, something competition couldn't feed any longer."

The next year she had to choose between returning to the World Longboard Championships or working the Triple Crown on the North Shore as a camera operator. She chose the work, gave up her seeded spot, and hasn't done a sanctioned event since.

2008: YOGA

Watching that 3:54 edit on theinertia.com, there is no doubt Leah Dawson does a lot of yoga to be able to contort her body into the stretch fives, cheater fives, and Strauch Stretches, sometimes scampering to the nose directly on takeoff and holding that crouching pose with one leg outstretched for the entire wave.

Speaking to Anna Langer for Pro Chat on CoolerLifestyle.com, Leah explained how she got into yoga in 2008: "I was introduced to yoga in 2008 by my dear friend and mentor Rochelle Ballard, who surfed on the WCT for seventeen years."

She discovered that the pain associated with her shoulder tendonitis faded through practicing yoga and regained the power of the breath. She practices Shadow Yoga (a blend of tai chi and hatha yoga) and uses uddiyana bandha, a breathing exercise. She says, "Yoga has incredibly improved my surfing. Balance, positioning, breath, and awareness are all things that straight transfer from the mat to the board. I've also found myself incorporating yoga stances into my surfing." The most important lesson of yoga: "harnessing my chi, my prana; in Hawaii we call it *mana*." It allowed her to find that "my chi is centered on my board, my maneuvers become more powerful, my hips are in flow. Yoga has also made me more calm, and peaceful in the water as well."

SOUL TOW SOUL

Can a soul surfer be a tow surfer? Is it inherently unsoulful to use an internal combustion engine to catch a wave?

Leah getting in deep
Photo: Ricardo Estevez

Leah Dawson tried tow surfing—once—and didn't like it too much. Hawaii water cinematographer Larry Haynes towed her into about six waves on a really windy day for the most intense session of her life. She felt like a rookie behind the ski, in a much larger lineup, with speed she wasn't used to.

On one particular wave, Larry kept looking back to tell her to keep holding on. When he finally told her to let go, she was at nearly the bottom of the biggest wave she'd seen up close. All she remembers is grabbing her rail to take the huge wind chop that approached her. Afterward she felt adrenaline more intensely than she ever had before. She hasn't towed again since then. "There may be a time again in the future, hopefully with glassier conditions, but the common place of the paddle in lineup is appealing to me, and perfecting my style on pumping 8- to 10-foot Sunset is appealing to me and still feels like big, powerful waves for me."

If she gets comfortable surfing with style on these smaller waves, she might seek bigger surf in the future. "There are many paths I dream to explore in surfing."

2009: FILMING

Leah began working as a camera operator in 2009, filming the Triple Crown and the Eddie Aikau Big Wave Memorial at Waimea Bay. Since then, Dawson has worked on a number of other projects—some for other producers, some self-produced.

Her latest project, *Peanut Butter: A Love Story*, is a visual ode to a 70s-era, sun-blasted 6'8" single fin surfboard she found under a house on the North Shore.

After finishing the film, Dawson launched the Sea Appreciation Project, "a media initiative I created when I finished my short film *Peanut Butter*," Dawson said to GravityResearch.com.

I recognized I wanted to establish an ongoing project that I could continue making short films with, that expressed an underlying theme. Appreciation is the first step toward awareness, toward a shift in consciousness, toward more love, more gratitude, which leads towards sustainability. Media is so effective in our world, so I seek to inspire as many as I can to feel Sea Appreciation. In hopes to make daily decisions that support that state of mind.

One of the Sea Appreciation projects was called *Julune*, which was "my visual representation of living a dream come true," Dawson said to Shawn Zappo on surfandabide.com. "My goal was to reveal the gratitude I have for the ocean." She spent her twenty-eighth birthday traveling to the Mentawais, where she had the best surfing of her life over the course of two weeks. "*Julune* does its best to show that women love the barrel as well, and we feel connected and appreciative of the ocean in a magic, unique way."

With the Sea Appreciation Project, Dawson also hopes to make more surf movies about women, "and sharing this timeless thing that we all do," Dawson said to Aeriel Brown at readwax.com.

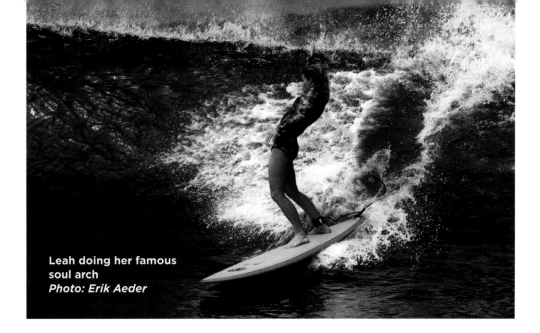

Leah doing her famous soul arch
Photo: Erik Aeder

I think it comes with the complete revolution in how we view women's surfing as a whole. What is that? What is that story? What is women's surfing? I don't care about just [filming] the best girl surfers in the world. I care about the mass of them, and what they are doing. What are they feeling? What are they connecting with? What inspires them? The door is so wide open. I'm really excited to walk through it. The main thing is to make media that girls can watch and go "Oh! I want to surf just like her."

Dawson also has issues with how women's surfing is marketed, and she hopes the Sea Appreciation Project will change that. "I think you have to stare it in the face," Leah told Brown. She points out that surfing has been a male-dominated industry that sexualizes women. "Does a woman have to wear a tiny bikini in order to look sexy in the water or to be a good surfer?" Dawson raises the questions that need to be asked.

GAME CHANGER

So that's the game, and that's how Leah Dawson wants to change it: through her own soul-powered surfing, but also by producing short films that showcase the sport's feminine side.

Mercedes Maidana, January 2016, on the east side of Oahu, at Kahana Bay, smiling in the face of adversity. The Argentinian charger suffered a serious concussion while competing at a big-wave event in Oregon in March of 2014. She's been dealing with the effects of that concussion ever since, but she keeps smiling. *Photo: Anna Riedel*

Born: May 13, 1981
Birthplace: Buenos Aires, Argentina

A CONCUSSIONARY TALE

Dying is easy. Living with a horrible health condition is not.
—*Mercedes Maidana*

LIVE FROM AUSTIN—AND HAPPY TO BE ALIVE

Mercedes Maidana was a big help with this book, as painful as it was for her to talk about surfing or think about the ocean, chiming in from Austin, Texas—far from her beloved Hawaii—where she is recovering from a serious brain injury suffered at Nelscott Reef in March 2014.

Concussions have been in the news and on the big screen lately, and Mercedes understands all this firsthand. A fairly standard collision with her board in 2014 has led to what could be lifelong repercussions—far beyond having to move from Hawaii to Texas and not surfing for nine months plus.

Mercedes has learned the hard way how to deal with and how not to deal with a concussion. So this profile will serve as a cautionary tale to all surfers and water athletes: Protect your head at all times, and if you are injured, take it seriously and be very careful to whom you go for help.

ROOTS

Mercedes was born and raised in Buenos Aires, Argentina, and lived there until she was 20. She didn't have much contact with the ocean, or with surfing. "I was a straight-up city girl. Grew up hanging around tattoo parlors, listening to punk and rock and roll, playing the bass in bands, and loving every bit about living in a crazy city such as Buenos Aires."

HEARTBREAK LEADS TO HEART'S DESIRE

At 18 Mercedes got involved with an older man, a famous Argentinian musician who was twenty-four years older. In 2001 they were in love and thinking about marriage, and then life whacked her upside the head. When Mercedes turned 20, her boyfriend suddenly left her for a famous actress. It was all over the magazines in Buenos Aires, which is how Mercedes found out. She was devastated and humiliated.

A sympathetic friend suggested that Mercedes get the heck out of Buenos Aires, where her heartbreak and public humiliation were staring at her from magazine covers. The friend suggested they take a vacation to Búzios, Brazil—a tropical peninsula northwest of Rio de Janeiro that is flanked by beautiful beaches. There is surf at Búzios, and that is where Mercedes's life changed. She tried surfing for the first time by herself, at 6 in the morning, with a board she borrowed from a friend. "As soon as I laid on the board I felt a rush of energy, as if a big ray of light was emanating from my body. For the first time in seven months, I was happy."

She had no idea what she was doing and nobody to guide her. She was tossed around trying to pass the waves to get to the outside. She didn't get up on the board once. "Yet I was ecstatic!" she recalls.

Mercedes fell in love with surfing that day. The one-week trip became a three-month trek along the coast in Brazil—from Rio to Fernando de Noronha, a tropical island in the Atlantic—alone, with a backpack and a board.

"As soon as I laid on the board I felt a rush of energy, as if a big ray of light was emanating from my body. For the first time in seven months, I was happy."

PURA VIDA

When Mercedes started surfing she was in her first year of college at a film school in Buenos Aires. She also started a leather business, which began with a bass strap and expanded.

Mercedes took many trips by bus to Florianópolis and Mar del Plata while in school. After graduating, she dropped the leather business, grabbed her board, and hit the road: Costa Rica, Australia's Gold Coast, and Indonesia.

In Indonesia she met a surf photographer who kept telling her that she should go to Hawaii. He thought she seemed fearless and that she would fit well with the Hawaiian waves. She thought he was crazy and that she would drown on her first day there, but she went, arriving with $200, a surfboard, and a backpack. "When I landed in the Honolulu airport, I stepped out of the plane and felt a voice within that said, 'You are now home.'"

HOME SWEET HAWAII

She moved to Hawaii at the end of 2004, arriving a couple of days before the Quiksilver in Memory of Eddie Aikau event, which Bruce Irons won. "It was like arriving to a surreal Disneyland of surfing," Mercedes says. "I loved everything about it. I arrived to Hawaii very humbly, eager to learn everything from everyone around me. I soaked it all in; surfing with the legends right next to me on a daily basis was beyond a dream come true."

Mercedes's heart was still wounded, but she found healing in the danger, challenge, and excitement of big surf. The desire to surf bigger and more powerful waves led her to the North Shore, where her love affair with big-wave surfing started. "The more power in the ocean the more alive I felt. And of course I got my ass kicked right away in my first weeks on the North Shore. I had my first 10-foot set land on me at Jocko's, losing my board, being in the wrong spot, and climbing back through the rocks. Total disaster, total panic."

She found a place to live at Rocky Point, worked at restaurants, and started a housecleaning service. "I think that I've cleaned every vacation rental on the North Shore." As the years passed, she hired a few girls to clean and was running her housekeeping business, making decent money while she dedicated herself to big-wave surfing.

SUNSET OBSESSION

Sunset Beach should be classified as an addiction. This North Shore reef break is one of the most difficult, challenging, rewarding waves in the world—a tremendous amount of open-ocean power unloading on an archipelago of reefs that varies with tide, swell direction, and wind.

To be able to surf Sunset Beach at size is to be in top physical fitness and at the top of your surfing game.

Mercedes got addicted to Sunset Beach, mentored by Darrick Doerner, Bobby Owens, James Jones, Clark Abbey, Andrew Marr, and many others. She asked them questions about the swell directions, currents, lineup landmarks, equipment, buoy readings, training—everything.

After two winters in Hawaii, she started to surf Sunset Beach and discovered a hunger for big waves. She progressed from 6-foot waves to 8- to 10-foot waves,

Mercedes grabbing a rail and going at Sunset Beach. This was post-concussion. She shouldn't have been there, but she just couldn't help herself. "I was surfing at 30 percent of my energy. This is the kind of thing I shouldn't have been doing if I knew better."
Photo: Shannon Marie-Quirk

and two years later she decided to try Waimea. She set goals for herself for every season: "It was a passion that once it unfolded I could never stop."

She put in most of her time at Sunset. With no mentor in her early years, she had to pay her dues there. There were hardly any other women surfing Sunset consistently, and some of the men didn't want her there. But she kept at it, and as time passed they started opening a space for her in the lineup.

When Mercedes was 26, she set her eyes on the prize: She wanted to ride bigger waves, qualify for the XXL Awards, and be sponsored by Patagonia. "I started training, surfing bigger waves every season, learning as much as I could from the legends around me at Sunset Beach. I became obsessed with manifesting my dream."

REAL WAIMEA: 2007+

In Hawaii there's a place called Waimea Bay, where the best surfers in the world go after they have mastered Sunset Beach. Mercedes surfed her first "real" Waimea in 2007, which she considers a turning point in her surfing. As soon as she made

Mercedes at Waimea in 2009, one day after the Quiksilver in Memory of Eddie Aikau big-wave contest
Photo: Bidu

Mercedes dwarfed by her 10'6" Kyle Bernhardt gun. "My first Waimea gun was a $70 beater that was way past its day. Eventually I met a North Shore shaper, Kyle Bernhardt, and I just clicked with his guns. He made me my first proper quiver, including my first 8'3" Sunset and 10'6" Waimea guns, both purple with pink rails. To this day, I keep using them. They just WORK. I had other shapers try to re-create them, but they don't feel the same."
Photo: Mike Bresnen

it to the lineup, she got the biggest wave of her life to that point. An hour later the bay started to get bigger and close out. "I was so scared yet so elated! When I made it to the beach, I was totally high, in love with Waimea. That's when I knew I could do this."

In 2009, the morning after the 2009 Eddie, she got what she considers the most beautiful wave of her life. As soon as she made it to the lineup, a set came and a friend yelled at her to go. "I turned around without thinking and dropped into the most beautiful, green, steep wall of water I've experienced. The colors of my board—purple and pink—were amplified by the emerald green. It was just perfection to the senses. I felt that in that drop, all the technique I accumulated throughout the years came together in one moment."

TRAINING

Training for big waves is part of the North Shore lifestyle because the North Shore is warm and beautiful. There is a camaraderie among other surfers, all of whom are preparing themselves for the risks and rigors of riding big waves—not just paddling and standing and going, but prepping their bodies for the inevitable beatings and tumblings from wiping out, getting caught inside, having to swim for miles.

By studying what other big wave surfers were doing, from training to eating habits, and by studying weather and surf reports, Mercedes came up with her plan. Unless the waves were over 6 feet, she would train 5 hours a day. In summer she would paddle from Sunset to Waimea [about 3 miles as Google Maps flies] or swim about 2 miles from Sunset to Keiki and run the beach back home. She would ride her bike 10 miles to yoga class and bike back against the wind. When Sunset was big and unruly, she would body surf with her swim fins "to get used to the washing machine."

Her focus was to get her cardio to a peak level, to prepare her body to handle the lack of air and strong impact in the water. She also wanted to be able to surf 8 or 9 hours of big waves during the day. "But the most important part of training was that if I knew I was in great physical condition, my mind would come along for the ride and help me overcome my fears."

XXL AWARD

Seven years after she started surfing, four years after she moved to the North Shore and two years after Mercedes threw herself into big waves, she was nominated for the Women's Overall Performance Award at the 2009 Billabong XXL Big Wave Awards. She was nominated again in 2010 and 2011.

She never won the category, but she still felt like a winner. "I fulfilled most of my surfing dreams. I surfed all the big-wave spots that I dreamed of: Jaws, Puerto Escondido, Teahupoo, Waimea, Sunset, Mavericks, El Buey in Chile. I also got sponsored by Patagonia, and that's how I was able to travel the world chasing big swells for five years."

Mercedes had been surfing big waves for seven years when she chased a big swell to the Nelscott Expression Session in Oregon in 2014.

Mercedes at Puerto Escondido, on one of the waves that got her nominated for an XXL award
Photo: Jeff Munson

NELSCOTT EXPRESSION SESSION: 2014

In March 2014 Mercedes was one of eight women invited to participate in a big-wave "expression session" at Nelscott Reef in Oregon. Their heat was 1 hour, paddling into waves that were a clean, glassy, 12 to 15 feet. Not too hard, not too soft—just right. On her first wave Mercedes took off on a wave between Paige Alms and Andrea Moller. "I was in the middle, going right," Mercedes wrote from Austin, Texas. "The wave jacked up and the drop became vertical. I was pretty late, so grabbing the rail was the only way for me to pull it off backside. The wave felt heavy, reminded me of Mavericks. Once I made it to the bottom, the lip got me and took me under to a heavy turbulence. This was not the wave where I got injured. But it was a wave that spooked me mentally."

BACKSTORY: SWALLOWED BY JAWS

Ten days before the Nelscott contest, Mercedes suffered a wipeout at Jaws so horrible, she thinks she was still suffering from PTSD when she was in the water at Nelscott.

All of this is horrific, but Mercedes's description of the incident at Jaws is like a nightmare. She caught a smaller "insider" wave that had the wrong angle; it closed out in front of her, and she wiped out. She got beat a bit, but had the conditioning to shrug it off. She surfaced to find a huge set bearing down on her.

Two guys on PWCs tried to rescue her, but the surf was too big and dangerous. She took two waves on the head before a ski driver named Nano finally picked her up.

> Once I was on the sled, I told him to GO! The next wave was about to break in front of us . . . a 55-foot face. It was so ridiculously big to see a wave like that from the impact zone that it was almost like a joke. The waves that broke in front of me looked like waterfalls from my angle.

But the ski didn't move. Says Mercedes, "It really felt like it was a horror movie or a big nightmare that you can't wake up from and I was just a character in it. It was surreal."

She and Nano were both on the Jet Ski when the wave hit them. "The sound underwater of the metal crashing with the wave was like listening to a truck crash," Mercedes remembered. She realized they were going toward the cliff and that she could also hit her head with the ski, so she let it go. Even with her inflatable vest, she wasn't coming up. Miraculously Nano showed up next to her again with the ski working, pulling her onto the sled and back to safety.

Mercedes coughed water out of her lungs for a while after she was able to go back to the boat. She lost her voice for some time but then was "back to normal." She continued, "I was in a state of 'adrenaline high' for days, feeling that if the worse that could ever happen in big-wave surfing just happened, I didn't have anything else to fear. A stupid sense of invincibility took over me. Nelscott slapped me out of it in one blow to the head."

Mercedes went to Oregon for the Nelscott event before she was able to properly process the near-drowning at Jaws. She mistakenly believed that nothing could be worse than the dramatic episode at Jaws and that Nelscott would be "a piece of cake. Well, the ocean has its ways to put your ego in place."

MEANWHILE, BACK AT NELSCOTT

Ten days after getting absolutely smashed at Jaws, Mercedes was in the water at Nelscott Reef in Oregon. The surf wasn't nearly as big as at Jaws, but it was big enough to do damage. Mercedes caught that wave with Paige Alms and Andrea Moller and got bashed around, but then the real damage happened.

A bigger set than what they'd seen all morning came to them. She thinks the wave that got her was about 20 feet Hawaiian. (The Hawaiian scale of judging waves is generally bigger than the mainland scale.) She tried to outrun the wave by paddling toward the channel to the right, but she wasn't going to make it. There was an instant when the fear of drowning that she hadn't processed since Jaws came up full force. She froze, which had never happened to her before. "I feel that I was always able to manage my emotions in order to react when necessary."

This time her emotions got the better of her. Instead of bailing the board and diving deep under the set wave coming at her, she ended up parallel to the wave and being too late to dive it. She went over the falls and the lip of the wave landed her 10'2" gun on her forehead. "The impact was ridiculous. I had never felt a hit that strong."

BLACK THEN WHITE THEN RED ALL OVER

Everything went to black, then bright white stars, and then Mercedes was back on the surface. Blood on her face, she got swept up by the rescue team Jet Ski to get her out of the impact zone. There were live cameras pointing at her and blood covering her face. Knowing her mother was watching in Argentina, she made an "OK" gesture, even though she knew it was bad.

The emergency room doctor told her she had a "mild concussion." He glued the cut above her eyebrow and sent her back to her hotel. Hours later, while the other surfers were at the awards party, she started vomiting and asked one of the contest organizers to help her. He drove her back to the ER, where they did a scan and said her brain was "okay."

But her brain wasn't okay. She had suffered extreme shocks that were both psychological and physical—as any near-death experience is. "I wasn't close to drowning at Oregon," Mercedes said. "I didn't black out, and I got Jet Ski assistance right away. The problems started days and weeks later, when swelling in my brain started to get worse."

The extent of the damage and her troubles slowly revealed themselves after she returned to Hawaii. She started to feel fatigued. About a week later her body shut down. She didn't have the energy to walk or talk. She was lethargic, irritable, anxious, depressed, and not in control of her own body. "Every activity of my daily living became as hard as climbing Everest to me. . . . It was like I wasn't myself anymore, and every day was a battle."

ANNUS HORRIBILIS

In November 1992 Queen Elizabeth II made a speech to the Guildhall that looked back on what would not be one of her favorite years. "Nineteen ninety-two is not a year on which I shall look back with undiluted pleasure," Her Majesty proclaimed. "In the words of one of my more sympathetic correspondents, it has turned out to be an annus horribilis."

For Mercedes Maidana, this was her annus horribilis. Four months after her concussion, she and her husband decided to get a divorce. They had been moving in different directions, and the concussion was the last straw. "I can't blame anything on him; it's just what happened. We are good friends nowadays," she says.

Mercedes was in such an "emergency mode" with her brain injury and divorce that she didn't even realize she didn't have any help. With her family in Argentina, she was used to dealing with extreme situations without having them close for support. Her mother offered to come to Hawaii to help her or to have her go to Buenos Aires to heal, but she couldn't even make a decision like that.

A few of her closest friends made meals for her, but they had their own problems keeping them busy; Mercedes found herself more or less alone. "It was all one big blur of survival mode," she says.

WRONG DOC

The doctor who treated Mercedes for the first two years only gave her medications for side effects, but her brain wasn't healing. He never told her to stop surfing, change her diet, or try any other kinds of treatments, and she didn't improve. She continued surfing, aggravating her concussion over and over again. Every time she got tossed around, she would get dizzy, weak, and nauseated. Every wipeout made her feel worse for days.

In February 2016, after a nasty wipeout at Sunset, she knew she had to stop surfing. "As soon as I took the impact with the water, I felt like a big knife was stuck in my head. Pure pain." Her eyes were so heavy she could hardly open them, and she could barely walk from the beach to the car. She had to wait for the dizziness to subside before she could drive. "I cried the whole way home because I knew that it was the end of me and Sunset."

HERE TODAY, GONE TO AUSTIN

For someone who is addicted to surfing Sunset Beach but can't surf Sunset Beach because it might end her life, Hawaii is a difficult place to be. So, like Odysseus, Mercedes packed up her gear and moved inland, to Austin, Texas, "to get treatments that I couldn't get in Hawaii and to get my financial life in order, since the concussion threw me off financially." She has a new profession that she finds fulfilling: helping families insure their mortgages so that in case anything bad happens to them, their loved ones won't lose their homes. "I know by experience what it is to have an unexpected accident. If your life turns upside down, your finances will hurt."

Mercedes is improving with new treatments, but she still has headaches, fatigue, trouble holding a conversation, and pressure in her head. What *keeps* her focused is healing so that she can return to the life she wants in Hawaii. "I want to go back to Sunset and my beloved outer reefs. I can, and will, do it."

A NIGHTMARE BECOMES A DREAM

There is light. Austin, Texas, just opened a wave pool, and Mercedes can hear Hawaii calling to her, across an ocean and half a continent:

I have a dream and I am determined to work hard for what I want. . . .

I visualize my dreams with gratitude as if they were happening with joy and enthusiasm. I now have hope.

I see an image of myself in my mind, carrying my pink 9'6" quad with my right arm. Facing the ocean, my favorite outer reef cranking at 15 feet, clean, glassy barreling lefts. Timing the sets while looking at the rips. Trade winds are blowing gently as the sun slowly starts to come out.

The morning air is crisp. My heart is pounding hard, yet my breath is slow.

I'm ready to go. Today the impossible became possible.

> I visualize my dreams with gratitude as if they were happening with joy and enthusiasm. I now have hope.

Born: 1986
Birthplace: Sligo, Ireland

IRISH UP

If we could all make small change happen, then it would make a big difference.
—*Easkey Britton, from the Waves of Freedom website*

JAMES JOYCE, JOHN KEATS, C. S. LEWIS, MAEVE BINCHY, EASKEY BRITTON

Ireland is better known for producing great writers than great surfers, but in Easkey Britton we have both. Photographer Lucia Griggi suggested Easkey for this book, and the first communication with her was April 17. After some back and forth, on the Fourth of July, Easkey delivered a swelloquent essay that made the author's job easier—he chose to run it in her words, word for word.

GAELIC FOR "FISH"

My name, "Easkey" (or "Iascaigh") has its origins in the Gaelic for "fish." It's also the name of a world-class surf break on the west coast of Ireland. A right-hand reef-break next to the ruins of a castle. One of my parents' favorite waves. Imagine if I didn't like the water!

Easkey Britton at home in Ireland, snug on the couch with mother NC, father Barry, and cousin/tow-partner Neil Britton
Photo: Lucia Griggi

Easkey in all her beauty,
Waikiki, Hawaii
Photo: Lucia Griggi

Easkey on the North Shore, winter 2009
Photo: Lucia Griggi

It does make me wonder at the power of naming, and the importance of our *he'e nalu*, or surfing roots—understanding the influence that can have on us, on our decisions, on our story.

As a kid we'd go on family road trips to my namesake and camp next to the surf break. My little sister and I curled up between our parents in the back of the van, listening to the waves crashing on the reef. At first I learned about the reef, the swell, and tides from my time spent in rock pools observing what the sea left behind when it receded and watching them fill in as Dad timed his surf for the pushing tide. It wasn't long before I followed my dad out there.

Easkey is also one of the first places I learned to surf over reef and where I began to hone a taste for more powerful waves under the mentorship of the local and traveling regulars who camped out on the coast seasonally or full-time, adopting me as their own in the lineup, sharing their water knowledge.

Easkey about to paddle out
on the North Shore, 2009
Photo: Lucia Griggi

Easkey rinsing off, Waikiki, Hawaii
Photo: Lucia Griggi

DA CAT'S KITTEN

One woman especially became a great pal of mine, Linda Wilson, who I later came to learn was a girlfriend of Miki Dora's, although none of that matters when you're a 10-year-old. Linda would camp out by herself for six months of the year in her little green van. What struck me about her was her grace both in and out of that water. She had long flowing hair, a strong sense of self, and would paddle out on a board of her own design on her knees and pop with a wave, drawing the most beautiful lines. She always had lizards painted on her board, maybe to remind her of someplace warmer, and we became pen pals for years—meeting up every year on the reef at Easkey for more tuition on grace. It was easy to draw parallels between her and Rell Sunn. She had a wonderful air of self-confidence and independence, although I imagine it must have been lonely at times.

Now I can understand what a powerful thing that was, to meet and be mentored by an older woman who was living this, I suppose, bohemian lifestyle, but on her own terms, and how simply you could live and still be happy (although it's also lost on a 10-year-old how long it can take a broken heart to heal).

ROOTS

Mum's from Donegal Town, which is 20 minutes from where we live now (and always have): Rossnowlagh. Her parents had a caravan on the beach at Rossnowlagh where they'd hang out every summer. Despite her parents being dead-set against her going surfing—especially her dad—in her teens in the 70s Mum managed to get her hands on her first surfboard after saving up for years and borrowing money from her uncle.

One of her first surfs in Bundoran, she got hit in the head by my dad's cousin, Jack Britton, which left a big gash across her scalp. She went around with a beanie hat on her head all summer to try and hide it from her parents. Eventually when her dad, Liam Mundy, did spot her surfing in Rossnowlagh one summer's evening, instead of getting mad he finally understood. He got it when he saw her riding a wave and the joy she felt and I suppose the surprise of what surfing really is, that we're actually riding this far-away kinetic wave of energy on tiny bent pieces of plastic (my own dad's definition/description of surfing!).

Mum lived for years in that little caravan by the sea, and it's where Dad finally proposed to her when he stopped noticing only "the next wave" and finally

Easkey, hitting the lip at Rocky Rights, Hawaii
Photo: Lucia Griggi

noticed Mum in the water too! That said, he's still a total surf addict. Like any addiction, he has all the addictive tendencies that go with it. A so-called "good addiction" that I've inherited from him. But he has it worse, still does. Mum knew, it was probably why she loved him so much, but it also shaped the "rules" of their relationship to the point where surfing always came first. And Mum accepted that for a long time because she knew herself how powerful that calling is, and I suppose there are far worse things to be pulled into on the rural west coast of Ireland if you're not a surfer.

As cold-water surfers, what attracts us to those hard edges and wild elements? For me, I feel cold water is the ultimate leveler.

DEALING WITH THE COLD

I never really thought about Ireland being too cold, until I started to travel. I mean of course it was bloody freezing! And it was long before we had decent wet suits. In winter there was the issue of daylight. I had this strategy, where Mum would pick me up from school and during the 10-minute car ride home, I'd get out of my school uniform and into my wet suit so I'd be ready to jump into the sea at my local beach and make the most of the dying light. I don't know any other kid as obsessed about anything as I was about surfing. The beach would be deserted, not a soul, certainly no other kids. It would be getting dark, and Mum would flash the headlights trying to either find me or get me to come out. I eventually would and she'd have to peel the wetsuit off me because I'd be too frozen to use my hands. I'm very grateful we had an amazing open fire at home, still do. I'd practically sit in it as I tried to finish my homework, rolling the pencil between my hands to bring some life back into them and my wet hair always dripping onto my copy book.

Easkey thawing out some more in Whacky Whacky
Photo: Lucia Griggi

Easkey Britton at home, standing with her *very* pink shortboard, shaped by Luke Hart / Art of Trim. "Mum loves when I get a bright colored board so she can spot me in the lineup when we're all dressed like sealskin in our wet suits in winter!"
Photo: Lucia Griggi

The cold was more a blessing than a curse. It certainly helped with crowd control.

Now it's a thing: "cold-water surfing." As cold-water surfers, what attracts us to those hard edges and wild elements? For me, I feel cold water is the ultimate leveler. It strips us of all our pretense, stereotype, or swagger. It breeds authenticity and trust. Gender lines blur, and it becomes about our strength of character and willingness to embrace the unknown and build trust in each other. It takes us out of our comfort zone: We have to really want to be there, with nothing to prove, because the elements don't care who we are, if we're man or woman. Trust, patience, solitude, grit, and resilience. It's the same thing that first attracted me to big-wave surfing.

SURFING APPEALS TO INTROVERTS

I think it appeals especially to introverts, or those with a greater inclination toward introversion despite our apparent extrovert ways. It's where we can recharge, replenish, come back to wholeness, gather our true energy about ourselves after

Does Ireland have that many trees? Actually this is Vancouver Island, another cold-water surfing area in a different hemisphere entirely.
Photo courtesy of Easkey Britton

having given so much of ourselves in a world of constant buzz, noise, and communication. Isolation can feel like a gift.

The other thing about cold water, you can even feel your old scars again as your skin tightens against the cold. Again, maybe that's the nature of my upbringing somewhere so isolated, on the border with Northern Ireland, daily life woven through with The Troubles or the aftershocks from that era of sectarian violence and conflict that spilled over and between the borderlands as we worked toward the Good Friday Peace Agreement—that strong sense of place, resilience, and wild Irish weather that seems to shape our very identity both physically and psychologically.

COMPETITION

From about age 8 I competed in contests at my local surf club in Rossnowlagh, also home to the junior national championships every summer. It was a just fun thing to do with friends for the summer. I was very driven, but not just in competition. I'd rope my friends and family into fund-raisers I'd organize using the beach space to the max—I'd have car-boot sales selling all my toys, getting kids parents to bake for cake sales, and have sponsored paddle races, or surfathons: "Sponsor me to surf a wave/how many waves do you think I can surf in an hour?" Seriously!

THE CHERNOBYL CHILDREN'S PROJECT

These charity events were in aid of my passion project at the time, the Chernobyl Children's Project: a charity that funded medical therapy and exchange holidays for children who were victims of the Chernobyl nuclear disaster.

The Chernobyl disaster happened the same year I was born, and I met some of the kids who came to Donegal for respite and health restoration, same age as me, thin and pale as ghosts, many recovering from cancer treatment (or still suffering from it), others terminally ill despite their youth, and they had never even seen the sea. That blew my little mind. I'll never forget the impact of being in the sea for the first time when they came to my local beach at Rossnowlagh for a day. Looking back, it was a moment that firmly cemented my belief in the power of the sea to heal, to connect across language barriers, across cultures, and the power of play. Just the simple joy of it all and how it transformed, even if only momentarily, their emotional and physical well-being.

CHANNEL THE DRIVE

My relationship with competitive surfing was always a pretty dynamic one, with the inherent tensions that go with that dance. It was one way to channel my drive and give me focus . . . but mostly it was a way to find belonging with a community of like-minded surfers. And most importantly, from the point of view of a young Donegal girl, it was a gateway to travel—an opportunity to get out into the world. My inner nomad and restless soul rejoiced, but my sense of self was conflicted. My dad is what many would refer to as a "soul surfer." He lives to surf. Surfing comes above all else; you do it because you love it and that's it. There should be no rules, only total freedom of expression (no surprise my dad is also an artist), and competition goes against the very grain of why we surf, in his opinion. And I understood that; a huge part of me believed the truth in that. But I also wanted more. I was hungry to learn, to push my abilities, to test myself, to meet others, for new experiences, to explore new places. At first I thought the competitive pathway could offer me those things and for a while it did . . . but then my horizons began to expand much farther beyond the confines of the commercial surf industry and I hated being in a bubble.

TURNING POINT 2010

Unsurprisingly, events began to converge all around the same time that started pulling me in different directions. The year 2010 was a pivotal period in many ways, very much like the early stages on Joseph Campbell's "Hero's Journey," responding to "The Call to Adventure"; a new journey of exploration through knowledge and education, starting a PhD/doctorate in Environment and Society; a sense of adventure and boundary-pushing in the surf in a new way—surfing Mullaghmore; and making that trip to Iran (God knows how the planets were aligned that year!).

SURF IRAN

It's one of the most common questions I get asked: "What made you want to surf in Iran, and what was that like?" I was coming out of an intense period of competitive surfing, had just begun my PhD. My sponsors at the time didn't support me to go. I think it was fear of what Iran represented, and a lack of belief in what was possible. Initially for me it was simply the sense of adventure, the pull of a place so unknown to me, and shock at my own ignorance of such a complex, historically rich, and highly politicized part of the world. I was invited to be part of that first trip by a surf photographer/travel writer through a mutual friend who proposed the trip.

Were we perpetuating the neocolonial surf travel myth of the "discovery" of empty, unexplored waves? Maybe. And yet, in the end we were two women, one with her surfboard and one with a small film camera (French filmmaker Marion

Gidget goes Iranian: This is Easkey leading a women's surfing workshop at Ramin Beach, Sistan-Baluchistan province, Iran. "That's me surrounded by Iran's next gen of female surfers (?!)." Next gen? First gen?
Photo: Jelle Mul

Get hijab: Local girl Parveneh's first surf, with Easkey, Mona Seraji (one of Iran's pioneering first women-of-surf), and local up-and-coming surfer Shams Fuladi, teaching the kid in the background.
Photo: First female surfers of Iran, 2013, courtesy: Waves of Freedom

Poizeau)—the only two to make it. We were on our own. It was an opportunity to confront my own assumptions about a very misunderstood part of the world. And we did find surf—in the remotest part of Iran, Sistan-Baluchistan, another "borderland" region next to the border of Pakistan. Marion and I were the first to have brought the female-led surf story of Iran into the public domain. It's been an unexpected and ever-evolving journey since—the story of the first female surfers of Iran, the cross-cultural impact of surfing, the mixing of not just gender but social class, religion, and ethnicity, is well documented in Marion's award-winning documentary *Into the Sea*, filmed in 2013.

IRAN'S FIRST FAMILY OF SURF

Every summer since, it's been a collaborative process co-organizing surf workshops with Marion, Mona, Shahla, their network of action sport enthusiasts from Tehran, Iran's first family of surf the Fuladis, and the local Baloch community at

Ramin Beach. It seems surfing is there to stay now. And it's certainly got under my skin. This year there has been a shift with a move to formally recognize surfing as a sport in Iran. I still find it kind of unbelievable. It's also interesting to see how it will go from here. I feel part of the magic and openness to such a diverse social mix lies in the play-like qualities of surfing rather than the competitive. With formalization comes regulations, rules for how it can and can't be done. Regardless of where in the world surfing takes hold, that dance always seems to emerge between surfing as art/play and surfing as sport/competition . . . our (human) need to control, even in an environment as untamable as the sea, never ceases to amaze me.

At a deeper level, I suppose why these places draw me (Mullaghmore, Donegal, Baluchistan) is because they represent the "borderlands," both in the physical and geopolitical sense, but also how we might bridge the worlds between self and society.

Shakespeare describes this scene well through Cassius in *Julius Caesar*: "Why, now, blow wind, swell billow, and swim bark! The storm is up and all is on the hazard." Easkey at Mullachmore, Ireland: as big, cold, heavy, dangerous, and exciting as it looks.
Photo: John Carter

BIG-WAVE EVOLUTION

It was never a "plan," like a lot things in my life. It wasn't like I clearly laid down the goal: "I want to be a big-wave surfer." It came about through a combination of timing, being at the right place at the right time, a lifelong sea-obsession, growing up around heavy water, knowing the right people, and luck.

THE BROTHERS MALLOY

In 2007 the documentary *Waveriders* was being filmed in Ireland. I got a voice-message on my phone from Chris Malloy saying they were in County Clare and going to surf the Cliffs the next day. I'd heard the stories about Mickey Smith and some of the local lads pioneering this crazy wave, Aileens, that winter, but I hadn't seen it with my own eyes yet. My phone went off again. It was big-wave surfer and local hellman Peter Conroy, who talked me out of driving back to university and into coming down to Clare instead. It didn't take much persuading! I still had no intention of actually surfing it. I was part of the water-safety crew in the channel, floating there for hours watching the most stunning waves I'd ever seen in my life. It was like falling in love, an intoxicating feeling of wonder and mild terror at losing control of yourself. And that was just from watching it!

It wasn't until near the end of the session, the light was starting to fade, Jet Skis were running low, that surfer Dylan Stott came and said, "Right, Easkey, let's go!" I didn't really have time to think about it. Chris Malloy threw me his oversized impact-vest; the straps on the tow board were too loose. I'd never done this in my life. In many ways I was totally unprepared, but then—what better time to do it when you're not overthinking it and you have some of the best watermen in the world and plenty of watercraft to haul you to safety? The adrenalin-hit was instant. Every sensation was so new, every fiber of my being buzzing. You have to imagine the setting: one of the most powerful natural amphitheaters in the world with some of the world's tallest sea cliffs rising up before you, a wall of water rushing up behind you, seabirds dive-bombing all around, spectators like ants on the clifftop. . . . I was giddy for days.

GEARING UP

It took a few years before I could find a willing partner in crime. No one was paddling these spots yet (although I did paddle Aileens in 2011 and famously snapped Fergal Smith's board). And surely there were more spots to be found? Finally I strong-armed my cousin Neil into going halves and buying a Jet Ski.

Mullaghmore became our training ground, so we had to learn hard and fast! And I learned everything, same as any of the lads. It didn't matter I was the only woman—I had to learn how to haul unconscious adult bodies out of the water same as the rest if it ever came to it. We had to have that level of trust in each other and understand how we all worked together. I loved that teamwork aspect to it, and we became the founding members of the Irish Tow Surf Rescue Club. Tow surfing in Ireland evolved initially from the need to explore, and a huge issue was accessibility and the nature of the waves themselves; now they have become a fundamental part of surf rescue.

GOOD THING ABOUT IRELAND

The good thing about Ireland is that there are still those days that catch everyone by surprise, where you have to be there patiently waiting and ready to jump for that window of a few hours between storm fronts with just a handful of friends in the lineup and my Mum (God love her) on the headland, bearing witness through her camera lens. An unexpected moment of magic where the elements align and it goes unnoticed but for a few mad souls taking their joy from it.

The standout moment is December 21, 2013, winter solstice. It's moments like this when it feels selfless, because a force so much greater has stripped us of all identity, gender or otherwise. A nameless wave can change everything in an instant, mirroring our greatest hopes and fears. There was only a handful of us, two skis, myself and my cousin Neil, our pals and big-wave chargers Barry Mottershead and Dylan Stott, and photographer Christian McLeod. We took it in turns, running safety for each other. It was close to sunset, the light was soft and golden breaking through the clouds, and the wind died while the swell peaked

**Easkey and her boards,
North Shore of Oahu, 2009**
Photo: Lucia Griggi

When Irish eyes are smiling, it sometimes means they are in Hawaii.
Photo: Lucia Griggi

just before dark. The biggest waves I'd ever been out in. I can't explain why, but it's the moment I felt like I finally belonged out there. I was right where I was meant to be because it reinforced why I did it—to be so fully present in such intense nature, to be part of that movement of energy, to experience the joy of that. To go to the edge, that borderland where sea meets rock, and find my aliveness.

CONSTANCY

I realize the need for constancy, the constancy that is balance—both holding on and letting go as Vessa, a circus friend of mine, said. If anything pulls me it's this clarity—trusting in the process, which for me is less about trying to change things and more about how we choose to be with the way things are, a lot like the act of wave-riding. A process of reclamation is under way to understand surfing as the feminine, sensual, multisensory, and reciprocal experience that I feel it can be.

ALANA BLANCHARD

Born: March 5, 1990
Birthplace: Kauai, Hawaii

BORN THIS WAY

NATURAL BEAUTY

In February 2014 Australia's *Newcastle Herald* explained who Alana Blanchard is and detailed the debate over whether a young pro surfer should be admired for her carving hooks or her physical looks: "SHE was voted No. 1 woman in the last international surfing polls, has more than 1.6 million followers on social media, a long list of sponsors, and *Forbes* magazine judged her one of the world's 30 most influential sports stars under 30." The article went on to explain that while Alana is considered by many to be the most popular surfer, she's done it without winning an event on the elite tour.

She's been featured in the *Sports Illustrated* swimsuit edition and has become the hot topic on the issue of sexualizing women's surfing. But Carissa Moore said it best: Blanchard "brought thousands of eyes to our sport by wearing her small bikini bottoms. I just want everyone to appreciate that she is an athlete as well and she takes what she does seriously." In fact Blanchard feels that you should wear what you're comfortable in, and she's happy with her choices. Although she is also a model who even designs her own swimwear for Rip Curl and stars in the web TV series *Alana: Surfer Girl*, surfing remains her priority.

Five-time world champion Stephanie Gilmore said Alana should be noted as the amazing athlete she is. "Alana is a great surfer; she's a fantastic surfer. I think she would be a little bit bummed that maybe her beauty gets more attention than her actual surfing talent. She's one of the most talented surfers in the world, and she's beautiful. For me, she's just capitalizing on her strengths, and good on her."

Alana Blanchard in Portugal
Photo: Lucia Griggi

CAN SHE SURF?

Can Blanchard surf? Go to one of her 482,000 Google hits (Bethany Hamilton got 545,000), hit "VIDEO," and you will see for yourself.

Matt Warshaw described Alana's surfing like this in *The Encyclopedia of Surfing*: "Lean, fit, and flexible, the regular-foot Hawaiian was a top-drawer talent by the early 2010s, surfing fast and smooth, her long arms elegantly punctuating swooping carves and the occasional aerial blast."

Remember, Alana is a Kauai girl, from the same talent pressure cooker island that produced Keala Kennelly, Rochelle Ballard, Bethany Hamilton, and a whole bunch of hot dude surfers. Alana's Kauai contemporaries aren't going to let her get away with being just a pretty face. And she's not. Alana can surf. She is a regular foot and has a smooth, flowing style. She surfs with speed. She surfs with grace.

So she makes it look good. So what?

Alana taking to the air in Portugal
Photo: Lucia Griggi

Alana getting ready for a surf
Photo: Lucia Griggi

You can see for yourself on *Alana: Surfer Girl*, which the networka.com web-site describes like this:

Alana: Surfer Girl—Pro surfer Alana Blanchard invites you to hop on board as she travels the world in search of waves and adventures. Hang out with Alana as she lives the dream.

  Surfer Girl gives viewers an inside look at the life of Alana Blanchard. And what a life it is. Blanchard grew up on the beautiful Hawaiian island of Kauai and journeys around the globe competing and surfing at beautiful beaches. She has even been featured in the *Sports Illustrated* swimsuit issue. Blanchard's success is the result of hard work and the support of a tight group of friends and family. Hang out with Blanchard as she lives the dream.

ROOTS

Alana's dream began on the island of Kauai, where she was born to traveling surfer Holt Blanchard and his wife, Sydney. According to Bethany Hamilton's father, Tom, "Sydney [Alana's mother] and Bethany's mother, Cheri, both loved to surf, so they brought all of their kids up surfing." Alana began surfing at 4 years old, began competing at 9 years old, and at 13 was a witness to history when her friend Bethany Hamilton lost an arm to a tiger shark while they were both surfing at Tunnels. Alana was by Bethany's side from the attack, to the long paddle to the channel and on the beach, keeping an eye on her friend and talking to her in case Bethany lost consciousness. She signed with sponsor Rip Curl at 14, "for her talent but no doubt her looks too," wrote Sam Haddad on theinertia.com.

COMPETITIVE ROOTS

At 15 years old, Alana showed the world she was more than a pretty face when she won the 2005 T & C Surf Women's Pipeline contest—beating some of the world's best surfers at the world's most dangerous wave.

As a competitor, Alana first surfed on the World Qualifying Series in 2008, competing in thirteen events, with her best finish a third place. She qualified for the World Championship Tour in 2009, and her best finish was winning the Women's Reef Hawaiian Pro in 2009 at Haleiwa—a specialty event at the time but all the participants were WCT tour surfers. She also finished fourth in the World Cup at Sunset Beach. In 2010 she was back on the World Qualifying Series grind, with her best placing a fifth in Portugal. Back on the WCT again in 2011, Alana put up a string of unlucky thirteenth placings, with a ninth at the Billabong Rio Pro. That put her back on the WQS for 2012, where she qualified for the WCT in 2013. She started the year with two fifth placings at events in Australia, and that put her on the WCT for 2014, where she again put up a string of thirteenth placings. In 2015 she competed in two WQS events; as of this writing, she had competed in only one event in 2016.

Kind of looks like she is over the competition thing for now, after going back and forth from the WQS to the WCT. She made $226,825 in prize money, and her endorsement money from Rip Curl, Reef, SPY Optic, Sticky Bumps, GoPro, Rockstar, and Channel Islands Surfboards probably also paid some bills.

The camera loves her.
Photo: Lucia Griggi

BORN THIS WAY:
ALANA EXPLAINS/DEFENDS HERSELF

This is how Alana Blanchard explained/defended herself to Brad Melekian from *Surfer* magazine:

This is what's comfortable. Think about it like this—this is my job. If I went to a regular job, if I was a secretary or something, I'd want to look good. I'd dress up for that part. I like looking cute. So I want to look cute in the water. Because I'm a girl. Female athletes have bad reps of being butchy and all that. I just thought, "I'm going to be a girl and see if I can do this." It's probably half the reason I'm here. Not necessarily because I'm wearing little bathing suits, but because I actually wanted to be a girl. I wanted to be feminine.

Alana watching pre-heat competition
Photo: Lucia Griggi

Think about the top performers in the world. Look at Beyoncé. She's wearing these tiny little outfits, and everyone wants to see her sing because she's looking amazing. Why can't we? We want to look cute too. Rihanna is wearing tiny little things. Not that we're Rihanna and Beyoncé, but they look hot, so why can't we? Just because we're athletes?

I don't mind it. I always look up to girls like Beyoncé, or Anna Kournikova. Girls who do something well but also look good. I think every girl loves to feel sexy and, sure, there's some creeps out there, but I'm putting myself out there. I guess I'm just working with what I have. I never knew that people would be so focused on that, but if they are, then that's their choice. I just want my surfing to show too.

Tom Hamilton has seen both his daughter and Alana evolve. He knows and understands Alana better than most. "Alana has always been a great surfer because she loves it. She is quiet and a peaceful person . . . she has an amazing boyfriend and loves her dogs. Both girls love their families and live modestly. [They] own modest homes and cars. No bling for them. They like to buy artistic shell jewelry, not gold. But mostly they are still passionate about surfing."

Passion. That's what it's all about, whatever you do.

If I went to a regular job, if I was a secretary or something, I'd want to look good. I'd dress up for that part. I like looking cute. So I want to look cute in the water. Because I'm a girl. Female athletes have bad reps of being butchy and all that. I just thought, "I'm going to be a girl and see if I can do this."

Bianca Valenti with her beloved pink Pyzel gun, up on the cliffs overlooking her beloved Ocean Beach, on what looks to be a summer day
Photo: Sachi Cunningham

Born: October 28, 1985
Birthplace: Los Angeles, California

COLD SWEAT

I believe that the mind-set, skill set, and tool kit big-wave surfers possess and how they use it to approach life puts them into a category of being "superhuman." I love superheroes!

—*Bianca Valenti*

OCEAN BEACH IS LIKE A BOX OF CHOCOLATES

Ocean Beach, San Francisco, is a scenic, historic, lively, and exceedingly treacherous place to surf. A world-class place to get your ass kicked, nearly drown, break your board, and spend an hour paddling furiously to accomplish nothing more than get swept a mile down the beach—from where Playland *used* to be to where Fleishhacker Pool *used* to be. Take fifty waves on the head and catch bubkes.

For surfers, Ocean Beach is like a box of chocolates: You never know what you're gonna get. The Beach—as the locals call it—has myriad moods, an endless alchemy of wind, fog, clouds, tides, currents, and swell direction.

When Mark Twain (or whoever it was) wrote, "The coldest winter I ever spent was a summer in San Francisco," he must have been sitting at Java Beach on Judah Street.

Even when the surf is small, the ocean along here is in motion. And when the surf is 8 feet or bigger, Ocean Beach can be one of the most treacherous places to surf on Earth. Just getting off the beach and out the back requires a combination of patience, science, knowledge, luck, and true grit.

Yes, it's as frickin' cold as it looks. Bianca Valenti charging the seasonal offshores that blow straight outta the Arctic (or so they seem). Hats off to Sachi Cunningham for swimming out to get these images.
Photo: Sachi Cunningham

LONGBOARD GAL

So how did a longboard gal from the relatively placid waters of Dana Point end up subjecting herself to the guaranteed dirty lickin's of Ocean Beach, San Francisco? And how has she evolved into one of the leading big-wave women, unsponsored, determined to raise the level of women in big-waves on all levels—personal and professional?

In February 2015 Bianca was interviewed on www.surfermag.com and described as "one of those iron-willed chargers" and "an almost criminally unknown member of the female big-wave surf community." In fact she has won the 2012 SeaHawaii Women's Pipeline Pro and the 2014 women's big-wave event at the Dive N' Surf Pro Nelscott Reef. She is a Mavericks regular, and she has no sponsors. Surfermag.com nailed it: "If you should ever find yourself sipping a coffee while safely perched up on the dunes overlooking Ocean Beach on the biggest Outer Bar days, Valenti will be one of those specks you see bobbing halfway out to the Farallones, hunting down the hulking beasts."

ROOTS

Bianca learned to surf in the grubby waters of Doheny and grew up in Dana Point. She first stood up on a boogie board at 7 years old, and her mom thought she might like surfing. Mom gave Bianca a budget of $100 to buy a board, and at Killer Dana Surf Shop in Dana Point she saw one of Kelly Slater's hand-me-downs for $125. "I wanted it so bad," Bianca said. "I already had his poster up in my bedroom reading '1992 World Champion Kelly Slater' in a huge Backdoor barrel."

But Mom said that was a budget-buster, so she settled for a $75 board covered with a skull-and-crossbones deck pad. The surf shop guys removed the scary stuff, and Bianca was off and surfing. She spent hours and hours catching tiny inside waves and having a blast. She begged to go to surf camp and to the beach as much as possible. Says Bianca, "My mom sat in her chair at the water's edge and said, 'You better not get into trouble out there, because I'm not coming in that dirty water!'" But her mother really supported the joy and passion her daughter found in surfing. "I feel so blessed to have such a supportive, awesome, non-surfing surf mom."

Bianca spent her formative years competing in Club Longboard events as a member of the Doheny Longboard Surfing Association—traveling up and down the coast to events with other families. As a teenager she competed in the United States Amateur Surfing Association, sponsored by Steve Walden Surfboards, Toes on the Nose, and Body Glove. "I really enjoyed competing and usually winning," Bianca said.

School was the priority, but Bianca also traveled to exotic locales. She competed as an amateur longboarder until she was 16, when she got burned out and started shortboarding. "I got a couple of barrels and then started looking for bigger and bigger and more and more of them."

WELCOME TO OCEAN BEACH, NOW TAKE THIS: 2005

The quest for bigger and bigger and more and more took Bianca north, across the Point Conception line, to Ocean Beach. Her first experience with The Beach was in 2005. Bianca and a friend paddled out on tiny, 6'1" surfboards on a big day. They somehow made it out, only to get caught in the worst possible place. "We got caught on the Outer Bar right in the impact zone of a 20-foot-face, hollow Backdoor-esque gnar wave."

Bianca and friend got clobbered in a way that only Ocean Beach can clobber someone—holding you down and slapping you like you owe it money or voted Republican or something. "I mean, I got pounded," Bianca told Justin Housman on surfermag.com.

Bianca experiencing the innermost limits of Ocean Beach
Photo: Sachi Cunningham

I was under the water just swimming and turning, and I opened my eyes and it was all dark, and I was slowly coming up to the top and I remember thinking, "If there's another wave, I'll die." But I came up and there wasn't another wave, thank God. I was gasping for air and my entire body was convulsing. I went in and stood in the parking lot and thought, "Man, I want to ride those waves." They were just so perfect, and you could have gotten the best wave of your life. And that was my new goal.

COMPETITION

Bianca tried professional competitive longboarding starting in 2006, but didn't dig it. "The first year they did the ASP Women's World Longboard Championship in Biarritz (2006), I got third," she said to Justin Housman at surfermag.com. "And then I never went back. It's expensive, and if you don't have sponsors, and none of the events are here at home, it's like, 'Do I want to spend my money traveling to longboard contests, or do I want to spend my money going to Puerto Escondido or Pipe?'"

Bianca graduated from UCSB in 2007 with a BS in global studies, with an emphasis in socioeconomics, as well as a minor in sports management. "I've always been passionate about sustainability, and the global studies program is largely focused on a sustainable future."

After graduating from UCSB, Bianca worked as a surf coach in Sayulita, Mexico, and took side trips to Pascuales—known for big surf. "I made friends with a native, Vanessa Gonzalez, who said, 'If you like Pascuales you will love Puerto!'"

Bianca did love Pascuales and spent the summer there until she broke all her boards, returned to So Cal, earned some money, went back to Mexico, and broke some more boards.

At Puerto Escondido she met Savannah Shaughnessy from Santa Cruz. "I knew Savannah surfed Mavericks, so I started asking her as many questions as I could, and I thought, 'Hmmmmm; I'd like to try that.'"

So she moved north—to get close to the power, get to know it, get to know herself in a way that Ocean Beach and Northern California demand.

Bianca going, going, gone! at Ocean Beach
Photo: Sachi Cunningham

THE OUTER SUNSET

The Outer Sunset is Surf City for many San Franciscans—close to the beach but mercurial in its many moods: beautiful in fall and winter, screeching windy in spring, depressingly gloomy in summer. Bianca lived 5 blocks from the sand, "Dead center of the beach, where the biggest waves are on a good swell!"

San Francisco was a hub for the gold rush in the mid-1800s and is now a hub for the "silicon rush" as billions and billions of dollars are being made in San Francisco and all through the area known as Silicon Valley. "Like big-wave surfing, living in San Francisco during the Silicon Rush is every emotion at once," Bianca said. Things move fast, and it's hard to balance wanting to do it all—surfing, training, work, and social life.

Not to talk shit and not sure if you include this, but there is definitely a unique (and often false) sense of confidence coming from successful techies who have become new surfers. So for those of us who have been living it for years, we are learning to navigate the lineup with them and respectfully impart the aloha spirit and teach what surfing etiquette is to these newbies. Most importantly, they try to teach safety—where they should paddle out versus where the experts go. The waters are getting more crowded, which old-time locals are salty about.

When asked what she does for a living, Bianca gave a very San Francryptic answer:

I'm an Italian wine specialist, restaurateur, human rights activist, and surf coach.

How often do you get to surf?

Every day.

How do you train?

Movement-based strength training with other world-class big-wave surfers and extreme athletes. Free-dive courses. Interval training, getting comfortable being uncomfortable. Surrounding myself with athletes like me.

How much did your conditioning improve?

1,000 percent, with an understanding of proper movement accompanied by mental training.

How did your equipment evolve?

I started off on equipment that was way too small! Then with the help of Nate McCarthy from Proof Lab, I got my first Mavz gun and started riding boards that helped me perform.

CHASING MAVERICKS

The usual Mavericks routine is to work your way up, surfing Ocean Beach, Steamer Lane, Scott's Creek, or other waves from Santa Cruz, north along the north coast and up to San Francisco. Get comfortable in 12- to 15-foot surf, be a strong paddler, find out if you can handle wipeouts in cold water, and then you are ready for the new Golgotha that is Mavericks—a wave that absolutely lives up to all the hype that's been placed on it since Jeff Clark let the world know about it in the early 1990s.

"The first time I paddled out there was three or four years ago," Bianca told Justin Housman at surfermag.com in 2015. "They were filming the Jay movie actually. It was a huge, glassy day, with some 30-foot faces. I was sitting out in the channel thinking, 'This is nuts.' But I ended up getting one on the wide bowl."

After that she thought she needed bigger boards with bigger dims then realized they were too big. "Now I think I have finally fine-tuned my gear so that it's right for me. My equipment now is focused on performing. I know I can catch big waves, and I want to perform with precision and control on those waves."

Bianca stays dedicated. "This year I've committed to surfing it every time it breaks. I want to get some bombs there. It's so challenging, and has so many faces depending on the conditions. It's a really confusing wave and can be a very counterintuitive place to surf. So many of the good ones look like they're beyond vertical, but then you see guys like Anthony Tashnick or Nic Lamb make it, so you know it's possible."

NAILING NELSCOTT

Bianca was paying her dues at Ocean Beach and Mavericks as women's big-wave surfing was bubbling—enough to warrant including a women's heat at the Nelscott Reef contest in Oregon.

Nelscott Reef breaks a half mile out to sea off Lincoln City, Oregon. Local surfer John Forse worshipped the wave from afar from 1989 until 1995, when he took a sketchy Zodiac inflatable out of the Siletz River and checked the wave out. He was paddling, he couldn't line the wave up, he almost got killed, and he realized Nelscott was one of those waves in what Hawaiian surfer Mark Foo called "The Unridden Realm": waves too big and powerful to paddle into.

Santa Cruz surfers Peter Mel and Adam Replogle cracked Nelscott by tow surfing it in 2003, and two years later Forse and friends held the first Nelscott Reef Big Wave Classic, on December 11, 2005.

NRBWC was tow-only until 2008, when a paddle-in heat proved popular and expanded the event to paddle and tow.

By 2010 the NRBWC was paddle only. Keala Kennelly won the Women's Exhibition.

Bianca got involved in 2014. She drove up to Oregon injured and, much to her surprise, came out a hero.

To make a long story short, Bianca was four months into rehab when she got an e-mail at 10 p.m. saying the Nelscott was green-lit for three days later. "I hadn't surfed in four months," Bianca said. "I immediately called my trainer and Mavs pioneer Lance Harriman and asked, 'Can I do it?' And he said, 'Well it's pretty risky and you could end up reinjuring and spending an extra six months rehabbing, but if it was me (him) I'd do it.'"

Bianca did it. She drove up with a crew of female rascals that included photographer Nikki Brooks, Savannah Shaughnessy, filmer Dayla Soul, and Jamilah Star. Injured, out of shape, new to the spot, unsure of herself, she still won the women's division of the Dive N' Surf Oregon Pro, competing against Andrea Moller, Keala Kennelly, Jamilah Star, Savannah Shaughnessy, Paige Alms, Wrenna Delgado, and Mercedes Maidana.

REALITY CHECK

Big-wave surfer Roger Erickson once famously said, "Everything's okay until it isn't." And that proved true for Bianca at Mavericks. She trained, she was ready—and it still beat her to within an inch of her life.

> Once you do the physical, technical, and spiritual training it takes to gain the confidence to try and go slay a Mavz dragon (the wave), you get hit with a hard reality check that there are fifty highly testosterone-driven, focused, gnarly, amazingly accomplished surfers out in the lineup in a 10–20-foot zone trying to do the same thing!
>
> It's very much like a watery zoo filled with hungry lions, so the crowd is thick. It's HUNGRY!

FAIR SHARE OF ABUSE

Bianca has a harrowing story of pushing through what she thought was a standard over-the-top at Mavericks. She tried to do a standard push-up on a slightly crumbling wave, but Mavericks is far from standard; she got sucked over the falls into the dead center of the impact zone. With a 30- to 35-foot face wave about to detonate, she caught a good breath and dove as deep as she could. She was held down a long time and came up to the next wave of the set. The same thing happened a third time.

HOUSTON, WE HAVE A PROBLEM

Feeling fatigued and with tingling sensations in her legs, Bianca decided to inflate her safety vest, which she was wearing for the first time. When she pulled the ripcord, nothing happened. She had assembled the vest incorrectly. She took two more waves on the head and then saw she was about to smash into rocks unless she acted quickly.

Bianca paddled to the rocks, jumped onto them, and jumped up off to narrowly escape the rock beating. Her throat was dried out, and she gasped for air. A friend and photographer on a Jet Ski asked her, "Did you just catch a wave and we missed it?" Says Bianca, "Nobody had seen my whole rookie mistake. It could've been bad."

Bianca's experience at Mavericks echoes Mercedes Maidana at Jaws and Nelscott, Keala Kennelly at Teahupoo, and Maya Gabeira at Nazaré. Indeed, most of the women profiled in this book have taken their fair share of abuse. Bianca has paid her dues, from surfing in ooky water at Doheny to getting worked on the Outer Bar at Ocean Beach to almost getting obliterated on the rocks at Mavericks.

Why does she do it? Because to be prepared for such beatings, and to be able to survive these beatings, means Bianca is strong—physically and mentally. Spiritually. And that kind of mind/body/soul fitness feels good. It makes life feel good.

What hasn't scared Bianca into moving to Fresno has made her stronger, and she is down for whatever the ocean has next. "It's an exciting time for the small but thriving surfing and women's big-wave surfing communities. There aren't very many of us, but the support, enthusiasm, and spirit are strong!"

Once you do the physical, technical, and spiritual training it takes to gain the confidence to try and go slay a Mavz dragon (the wave), you get hit with a hard reality check that there are fifty highly testosterone-driven, focused, gnarly, amazingly accomplished surfers out in the lineup in a 10–20-foot zone trying to do the same thing!

It's been inspiring to Bianca to see how the men's side of the sport has grown, and she's excited about continuing to create and grow the women's surf community. She sees women as catalysts of change: "We just started a nonprofit called SUPER SESSIONS dedicated to progressing women's big-wave surfing and doing social good, like providing mentorship to up-and-coming girls/teens who have the big-wave bug." They are also thinking of ways to progress and evolve the sport in new and exciting formats beyond the traditional one-day event.

Still, Bianca loves the one-day events. She's looking forward to the WSL's inaugural Women's Big Wave Championship Tour, beginning in October (2016). "You better believe I am going for the win."

This photo belongs on a velvet hippie blacklight poster being sold in Haight-Ashbury circa 1967. It's that cool. Bianca Valenti silhouetted by old Sol, Ocean Beach. *Photo: Sachi Cunningham*

Paige behind the wave
Photo: Erik Aeder

PAIGE ALMS

Born: April 6, 1988
Birthplace: Victoria, British Columbia

MAUI WOWIE!

Ha-ha, a junkie? That's a little much, but I do love getting my heart pumping! I actually play it pretty safe and smart, I think. You definitely have to have a little screw loose to be out there (Jaws) because it's just beyond crazy. I never thought I'd be out there paddling! Anyone who says it's not scary is totally lying; it's just working through that fear, and once you catch a wave you feel so accomplished that you're high for a month.

—*Paige Alms, in* FreeSurf *magazine*

On January 22, 2015, Maui resident Paige Alms fulfilled a dream when she paddled a 9'4" SOS gun into a clean 30-foot wave at Jaws/Pe'ahi. She watched as Albee Layer, Kai Lenny, and Nakoa Decoite all got out of her way by kicking over the top, then bottom-turned and pulled into a big, blue Jaws barrel. Paige made it look good. The wave was filmed from land, sea, and air; and being the first woman to pull into a barrel at Pe'ahi earned her a nomination for the 2014–2015 WSL Big Wave Awards. She ended up taking the win for the Overall Women's Best Performance that year alongside the other nominees: Keala Kennelly, Silvia Nabuco, Emily Erickson, and Jamilah Star.

Paige made it look good. Her entry and bottom turn were as clean as the barrel she pulled into and the exit she made to shaper/soul mate Sean Ordonez and friends freaking out in the channel. The ride was filmed by Dan Norkunas and Jace Panebianco on a boat nearby and later edited by Jon Spencer into an edit with Paige smiling as she narrated an experience she described as "beyond words." But her words were pretty awesome: "I had a really good feeling after being out there the night before and getting amped and watching the guys go crazy. It was like, 'Okay, today is the day. It's glassy. It's beautiful. We're gonna get really good waves.'"

She'd been surfing Pe'ahi since she was 17. It'd been a goal of hers since watching Albee Layer, and her confidence had finally returned, as had her strength. "I got to my feet and that new board that I have, there was no moment of flailing at the top. The nose felt like it just pulled me into the wave, and as I was bottom-turning I was like, 'Oh, my God, this is the one.' I know that feeling. The best waves I've ever got at Honolua were that same feeling. As soon as I tucked up under it, I was like, 'Oh, my God! You're in the barrel!'" She'd accomplished a dream. "The experience of actually achieving that dream for the past five years is just mind-blowing and I'm beyond words. I can't even describe how amazing it feels."

Paige turned 28 in April 2016. That is the prime age for any athlete, but big-wave surfers generally have longer careers in the surfing world, sometimes staying relevant into their 50s—even their 60s, like in the case of Clyde Aikau, who paddled out and caught waves at 66 years old during the 2016 Quiksilver in Memory of Eddie Aikau Big Wave Invitational.

ROOTS

Alms was born in Victoria, British Columbia, and at age seven left Canada for an adventure in Australia with her mom. After driving around Australia in a van for ten months, and taking her first surf lesson, Alms moved with her mom to Maui at nine years old. She began surfing a year later. By 13 she was winning competitions and then she showed a precocious interest in and talent for big waves: "I always loved bigger waves," Alms told Will Coldwell for the United Kingdom's *The Guardian*:

> The power, the energy. . . . My mentor, Chris Vandervoort, took me out to a Maui outer reef when I was 15. I remember being scared the whole time and slowly inching my way closer to catching a wave. I caught a few waves that day and had never felt more alive.
>
> That session was the first time a female surfer had paddled at that outer reef, according to all the guys who had been paddling there for twenty years.

Paige feeling the power about halfway through a perfectly executed duck dive. She's releasing pressure through her nose and about to pop through the back to see if something is coming.
Photo: Erik Aeder

Paige's first session at that outer reef was just the start of a path that led her to pulling in at Pe'ahi thirteen years later.

Paige eased her way into more big-wave sessions, tow surfing and paddling a few times at the outer reefs on Maui and then tow days at Pe'ahi when she was 18. "Tow surfing Jaws was always so much fun," she said. "Seeing those waves up close and then being whipped into them by a ski, I was hooked."

A few people had paddle-surfed the left at Jaws on bigger days for years, but in 2010 Ian Walsh and Shane Dorian proved to the world that it was possible to paddle into some really big waves on the right. In 2011 Paige joined the crew for her first paddle session at Jaws. All her friends were doing it—Albee Layer, Billy Kemper, and Matt Meola, to name a few—and she didn't want to be left behind.

My first session I rode a 10'2", caught three waves, and was just amazed at the power of the wave; it almost didn't seem real.

I was feeling pretty confident and paddled a little deep, then got caught inside and broke my leash. Luckily a friend showed up on a ski and gave me and Albee a ride in (as he had just broken his board a wave before). That day we all agreed to have a safety ski in the lineup if we were paddling. Sean and I bought a newer used ski two weeks later.

Overcoming the fear of riding big waves does not come easy and it is not always easy to push aside. In order to paddle into big waves, you have to overcome your fear of paddling out, your fear of paddling for one, and the fear of falling on a wave. I can't describe how I do it; it's just a feeling that you push through in hopes of finding the rewards or memories of a lifetime.

I have had a challenge with switching my confidence on for big sessions ever since I had a severe shoulder injury in May 2013 while surfing in mainland Mexico. When you get injured like that and are kept out of the water for a long period of time, you look at things—and especially big waves—a little differently. In the winter of 2014–2015, I had figured out how to get my *mana* (Hawaiian for a power or life energy) back for those sessions. After three or four amazing sessions that winter, on January 2015 I caught the wave of my life at Jaws.

BIG-WAVE DANGER IS NOT A HOAX

Big-wave surfing is dangerous. Talk to Rochelle Ballard, who has suffered more injuries than a rodeo cowboy. Or take a look at the photos of Keala Kennelly after she face-planted into the reef at Teahupoo on Tahiti in 2011. Kennelly nearly lost half her face in that accident, and could have died from shock or loss of blood if the rescue people hadn't been on top of it.

From the 1940s to the 1990s, very few serious big-wave surfers were gravely injured or killed while riding big waves. Then in December 1994 the surfing world was shocked when Hawaiian surfer Mark Foo drowned while surfing Mavericks in Northern California.

Exactly one year later, on December 23, 1995, Californian Donnie Solomon drowned while surfing Waimea Bay on Oahu's North Shore.

Paige in the barrel at Pe'ahi-aka Jaws. This isn't done often by anyone, and Paige was the first female to solidify her name on the list.
Photo: Erik Aeder

In February 1997 Todd Chesser—a fit and experienced Hawaiian big-wave surfer—drowned while surfing a North Shore outer reef called Alligator Rock. Chesser knew what he was doing, he was with friends who knew what they were doing, and the ocean still took him.

In 2005 Tahitian surfer Malik Joyeux—who had survived many things at Teahupoo and the reefs of Tahiti—suffered what looked like a standard wipeout on an 8-foot wave at Pipeline. The wave broke Joyeux's board instantly, and when he didn't come to the surface, every surfer in the lineup spread out, searching the reef for color. Joyeux was found floating unconscious at Pupukea sandbar. Efforts to revive him failed.

On December 4, 2007, Carmel surfer Peter Davi drowned while attempting to paddle into a giant day at Ghost Trees, a wave that breaks along 17 Mile Drive in Carmel. Davi was attempting to paddle where others were towing. He moved to the inside and either wiped out or got caught inside. He was found floating in a pile of kelp, and efforts to revive him failed.

On March 16, 2011, Hawaiian surfer Sion Milosky wiped out on a big wave at Mavericks and was held down for two waves. He was found floating facedown a mile away, near the entrance to Pillar Point Harbor.

For most of the twentieth century, surfers dying in big waves were extremely rare. But into the twenty-first century, serious injuries like Keala Kennelly at Teahupoo, near drownings like Greg Long at Cortes Bank in December 2012, and deaths have become a part of the pursuit.

Paige Alms is aware that big waves are dangerous and can be deadly, and that knowledge powers all her training sessions, her time in big waves—everything from what she eats for breakfast to how she sleeps at night.

TRAIN FOR PAIN

While surfing Mexico in May 2013, Alms suffered her worst wipeout. "I was in Mexico, and I dislocated and fractured my shoulder in May," Alms told *FreeSurf* magazine. "I got lipped by a 10-footer on my head, and my shoulder popped out. It was the worst pain I've ever experienced. I didn't find out it was broken until a week later back on Maui."

It took months of rehab to fix that shoulder, but physical training is a part of the game for big-wave surfers. They train their bodies not just to paddle for and ride the wave but also to survive the rigors of wipeouts in big surf.

That was the theme of the Hollywood movie *Chasing Mavericks*, and it's the theme of Paige Alms's daily life. "I think physically the best thing you can do to train for big wave surfing is surfing in general," Alms said to *FreeSurf* magazine. "Learning the way the ocean works, the currents, the bumps; especially here in Maui we have constant cross bumps from it being so windy. I also do a lot of training in the gym, just a lot of core strength and cardio."

Surfers who know they are going to wipe out and possibly be held down for two or three waves have to know they can hold their breath for as much as a minute. And a minute in turbulence and fighting for the surface translates to a few minutes in calm water. "I do breath holding, but I'm not religious about it. Most of it is mental and teaching your body what it's capable of. I was taught in a performance free-diving class that an average human being should be able to hold [his or her] breath for 4 minutes. It's like meditating—you put yourself somewhere else. It's mentally draining though; I'm exhausted by the end of it."

But even training in calm water can be hazardous. In June 2001 experienced big-wave surfer Jay Moriarity was in the Maldives doing breath-holding exercises by swimming 40 feet to the bottom, sitting in a lotus position, and meditating—training his body to conserve oxygen.

Moriarity broke the first, second, and third rules of diving by diving alone. Something went wrong, and Moriarity drowned—most likely from shallow-water blackout. A kid who had survived one of the worst wipeouts in the history of surfing at Mavericks—a wipeout immortalized in the movie *Chasing Mavericks*—ironically drowned in 40 feet of calm, tropical water in the Maldives.

Big-wave surfing has its obvious hazards, and its not-so-obvious hazards. But female adrenaline and challenge junkies like Paige Alms weigh the risks against the rewards, and sometimes the rewards can be rewarding to the soul—like that barrel she pulled into at Jaws in January 2015.

Alms didn't win the Ride of the Year Award for that XXL Awards, but she did win the Billabong Overall Best Women's Performance for the second time. The first was in 2011.

EL NIÑO LOCO

The El Niño winter of 2015–2016 went berserk in the Pacific Ocean and allowed the women to raise the bar on All That Had Come Before. Paige Alms was the first woman to pull into the barrel at Jaws, and that left her hungry for more:

The best part of 2015–2016 was watching everyone push themselves on the biggest, cleanest waves ever surfed at Jaws. I saw some of the most insane waves ever ridden and also some of the worst wipeouts. I had a pretty mellow winter myself, caught a few clean ones, but sat on the sidelines, as I had shoulder surgery at the beginning of October 2015, then pulled my

Paddle-surfing big surf in Maui is all about wind. The gusts are unpredictable, which can turn a sure thing into a disaster. Paige, late and deep at Jaws.
Photo: Erik Aeder

hamstring first session back in January. I had a few memorable sessions in March that I was stoked on, less crowded than the January swells :).

I have yet to find another barrel at Jaws, but every session I'm hunting for a bigger and better one! I've been traveling all summer and just got back from five weeks of getting pitted at Cloudbreak, pretty happy :).

What is she fiending for next?

I'm really looking forward to this coming winter, being in peak shape and no injuries! The sky is the limit when your body feels good and your confidence level is high.

Besides surfing Cloudbreak 24/7 for weeks on end, how is she training for the winter of 2016–2017?

I train at the Deep Relief Athletic Training Center 2 minutes from my house four to five days a week. I work closely with my trainer on a program that is specifically for me, how my body is feeling, and what the surf is doing. I'm so grateful to have an amazing team and to learn more and more about my body and what it is capable of!

Any equipment changes?

No need to change equipment when you have magic boards under your feet. I am going slightly shorter on my guns, that's about it. Top-secret kine stuff ;).

What's next for Paige? And what is next for women in giant surf?

My goals are to continue paving the path for the next generation and pushing my own limits. I would love to travel to more destinations and get more comfortable in different lineups. I see women's big-wave surfing progressing every session. It's heading in the right direction: skilled surfers completing rides!

[In November 2016, Paige applied her local knowledge to win the Women's Division of the 2016 Pe'ahi Challenge. In typically big, windy, impossible, challenging surf at Pe'ahi/Jaws, Paige tallied a score of 21.66, finishing first ahead of Justine Dupont, Felicity Palmateer, Keala Kennelly, Emily Erickson, and Laura Enever.]

Alison Teal, water warrior
Photo: Sarah Lee

ALISON TEAL

Born: May 8, 1985
Birthplace: Floor of a log cabin in Eldora, Colorado

THE ADVENTURESS

INDIANA JANE

On a surfing safari to Morocco in 2008, Alison Teal kissed a cobra to save her life. In a market in Marrakesh, Alison was approached by an insistent, self-styled faith healer from the Sahara Desert wrapped in blue and gold robes and topped off with an ornate turban bigger than a camel's hump.

Alison tells that the holy man solemnly intoned, "In your near future you will have a serious surfing accident. You will die if you do not kiss a live cobra immediately." She had just finished USC film school and was about to embark on a camel safari to surf the desolate Moroccan coastline, and decided it was better to be safe than sorry—or dead. Watch what happened on Alison's website under her film called *Snaked!*, and when you do, don't stop there because Alison is more than a surfing goddess, Hawaiian hula pro, Balinese temple dancing champion, world-class mountaineer, and extreme skier and snowboarder. She is also a globally recognized, award-winning eco-warrior for our threatened planet and is dedicated to saving our beautiful oceans and the world on which they provide tasty waves for surfing. She is a surfer with a mission. Her exposé of Trash Island in the Maldives island chain was reported by *Time* magazine, CNN, the *Huffington Post*, and all major television and media outlets across the world, and awakened the world to the environmental threat of global plastic pollution.

Truth has been stranger than fiction throughout Alison's life. In 2016 *Time* magazine called her the "female Indiana Jones," and *O, The Oprah Magazine* called her "the Oprah of Adventure." She is the daughter of one of the world's foremost adventure photographers—her father, David Blehert—and a venerated international yoga master—her mother, Deborah Koehn. They took her skiing with

Alison on her Alaia board
Photo: Sarah Lee

them at only two months of age on Ausangate, southern Peru's highest peak. Then it was on to trekking in the Himalayas when she was just beginning to talk in paragraphs, being walked over by a sacred elephant in Thailand, and entering a schoolroom for the first time at age six at the base of Mount Everest in Nepal. So it should come as no surprise that the foretold mortal surfing danger in Morocco actually did become a matter of life or death.

Anchor Point is the bland name for the most famous, and perhaps most hazardous, surfing break along the Moroccan coast, and despite the massive swells and strong winds that whipped the surf into froth that fateful day, Alison dismounted her camel and jumped right in with her signature pink surfboard, easily paddling out to a takeoff spot without concern. And then she was instantly wiped out by a vicious set and hurled, crashing into a jagged crevice in Anchor Rock itself, where a staggering crush of seawater threw her down, down, down into swirling blackness, gasping for air. There was a gunshot-like cracking noise that she was sure was the sound of her spine breaking. With what felt like her last whisper of breath, she saw the filtered light of a rainbow far, far above her, and swam up to it for what seemed an eternity before finally popping up through the churning surface foam alive. The crowd that had gathered rushed to pull her to shore before the next wave came in expecting to retrieve her lifeless body, not to be greeted by her with laughter and hugs.

When Alison sat on the beach and examined herself, she was amazed to find no injury, not even a scratch. Only a fin on her surfboard had been snapped off, and she realized that had probably been the source of that terrifying cracking sound. Was her safe return from certain death the predicted result of having kissed a cobra for protection or just incredible dumb luck? You decide. Alison has no explanation but admits to having had no doubts about surviving her deadly encounter with the killer sea even as her breath ran out. She doesn't know why she felt confident she would not die that day. You can guess about that as well.

Alison on her travels in Fiji
Photo: Lucia Griggi

A LITTLE GRASS SHACK IN KEALAKEKUA, HAWAII

Shortly after Alison was born, her family got an assignment from *Mountain Bike* to go on a photojournalist adventure around the Big Island of Hawaii and test some of the first mountain bikes ever invented. They came across an incredible piece of oceanfront property and decided to build their home base there. They called it "Hale Kai," or "Ocean House," and more than twenty years later their very own "Robinson Crusoe Style Grass Shack" has become a renowned yoga and spiritual retreat center, and Alison's beloved "dry land" residence.

When asked to list the countries and places she visited, Alison answered, "I saw most of these places before I was seven: India, Tibet, Nepal, Indonesia, Africa, Thailand, Peru, Bolivia, Brazil, Ecuador, most states in the United States, Dominica, St. Martin, Puerto Rico, all of the Caribbean, Israel, Egypt, Costa Rica, China, Japan, Korea, Australia, New Zealand, the Maldives, England, Germany, Switzerland, Belgium, Holland, Fiji, Guam, Dubai, Singapore, Spain, Mexico, Baja Mexico, Syria, Pakistan, Jamaica, Palau, Malaysia, Morocco, and Sri Lanka."

WORLD-SCHOOLED

As for her schooling, it's inaccurate to say Alison was "homeschooled" because she was rarely home, but let her tell it:

The world was my classroom and the ocean my playground. My ad-lib, free-form, on-the-move, literally homeless version of "homeschooling" took place on the back of a llama, under an elephant, in a tent in a blizzard on Mount Everest, on a camel safari across the Rajasthan desert, or wherever else on earth my adventure photographer parents' work took them. The world was my school and my playground. I lived out of a backpack my entire life, and what was and is "normal family life" for me is light-years away from most people's idea of normal. But it was the life I knew from birth until I first saw the inside of a schoolroom on the high slopes of the Himalayas in Nepal.

Sounds romantic, but my one dream growing up was to go to a normal school which handed out normal homework and picked me up, and took me home in a normal, big yellow school bus.

Alison at home with Mother Nature
Photo: Lucia Griggi

"I've never been interested in the learning curve," she says, "I just want to do whatever I love immediately. And that's a blessing and a curse."

As a tropical cyclone approaches, Alison Teal heads out in search of a secret surf break off the coast of a remote island in Fiji while shooting her film *Lost Island of the Fire Walkers*. *Photo: Lucia Griggi*

Alison surfing Cloudbreak
Photo: Sarah Lee

But even then, the siren call of the surf thrilled and beckoned me, the ocean's roar calling to me, its musical invitation to adventure somewhere between a lullaby, and a marching song for Navy SEALS on a mission.

PINK = PASSION

Alison's first board was pink. She's big on pink. "To me pink represents my passion for life, protecting the Earth, and keeping everything fun!" But her pink surfboards are "green to the core," made from recycled coffee cups and other Styrofoam remnants. Her pink bikinis are also made from recycled plastic bottles.

Alison's parents didn't start surfing until their 50s, so she taught herself to surf, with help from people they met on their travels. Unfortunately, their fishing village home in Hawaii wasn't known for surf, but when they started adventuring to more tropical locations, they all became "born-again surfers."

Alison surfed at a place on Bali surfers call "Dreamland," a popular stretch of beach on the Bukit Peninsula near Kuta Beach. As she began to fall more in love with surfing, her family decided to live in Dreamland for a while. She refused to learn on a longboard because she's so tiny and it felt like a lot of board to handle, so she would borrow shortboards and get slammed in the waves at Uluwatu until she could surf. "I've never been interested in the learning curve," she says, "I just want to do whatever I love immediately. And that's a blessing and a curse."

From the Big Island to Bali to Fiji, Alison's "world-schooling" also included "world-surfing." In 2008 she traveled to Fiji and lived in a haunted tree house at Tavarua for a month. Here she found her "true 'sealed deal' love for surfing, and graduation into a full throttle surfing life." Cloudbreak soon became her addiction and favorite wave on Earth. "I would surf from sunup until sunset—or when the doctor would pull me in because I literally couldn't see through my sunburnt eyes."

NEVER TOO LATE

Alison does inspirational school tours where she teaches kids that it's never too late to follow their dreams or master new skills. She does not buy into the concept of winning, and consequently has never competed in a surf competition, but surfing isn't about winning to her. "It's about passion and living life to its fullest." She believes she loves it even more because she's never felt pressured to stand in the winner's circle, and getting a medal for doing what she loves. Surfing is its own reward.

Alison also wants the world to know that surfing can be a vehicle to promote change. "A smile and a pink surfboard can open any door, and my lifelong dream has been to show that one girl with little more than a coconut and a pink surfboard can change the world and bring my love for the ocean and passion for reminding all people that we are one to everyone."

She's not sure where her innate and passionate love for surfing came from, but maybe it was meant to be. "It is no mistake the first surfboard—or *alaia*— which belonged to a legendary Hawaiian princess was discovered in a sea cave behind my house on the big island!"

For Alison, surfing is the one sport that sums up life. "Surfing is all about pursuing what you love, and committing to it 110 percent no matter what the outcome will be. Paddling hard and then letting go of control. When you go for a wave, you may get the ride of your life, or you may end up on the reef or you may end up discovering a whole underwater world you never knew about."

Alison's favorite places to surf are Tavarua and her home secret break on the Big Island, but she has been around. "I've surfed off the island of the fire walkers in Fiji and in Israel while majestic Arabian horses danced through the shore break. I've surfed the desolate coastlines of Morocco and Peru. I've surfed the most remote areas of New Zealand—riding to the sea on horseback and taking a few 'surfaris' across Australia. I've surfed multiple places in South and Central America, the Maldives, and most recently Sri Lanka, and I loved strapping my boards on a *tuk-tuk* [a three-wheeled rickshaw] each day and cruising the coast."

Where has she not been yet? "I want to go to Madagascar, Egypt, Tahiti, and Samoa!"

SUMMA CUM LAUDE

in 2008 Alison's immersion in indoor "normal world schooling" ended when she graduated surfer cum laude from the University of Southern California graduate schools of theater and film at the same time—with some extracurricular post graduate time at University of California, Berkeley.

I know what you're thinking: How did a young woman with almost no formal schooling get admitted to a prestigious school like USC? Is there a cobra you can kiss for that? The answer, Alison admits, "Is because I'm a nerd stuck in a surfer girl's body." She attended senior year at Hawaii Preparatory Academy on the Big Island and received a 4.6 GPA. The combination of her GPA and unique upbringing—and maybe some magic from every shaman she met around the world resulted in her being accepted into every university to which she applied, and applied her surfing "all in" philosophy to getting an education. "Because my number-one dream growing up was to go to school, I worked my buns off to get the absolute most out of it. That, and a family that believed in me plus a dash of some Hawaiian tribal pixie dust did the rest."

If you're wondering how a fanatic surfer chick, who spent the first two decades of her life living a free-wheeling, unstructured life from mountains to jungle would cope in the concrete jungle of central Los Angeles, relax. She loved USC and film school because it was filled with dedicated, creative overachievers with impossibly big dreams—just like her. At times however, she felt like a Hawaiian fish out of water, this homeschooled weirdo straight out of the movie *Mean Girls* striving to adapt to a classroom with four walls and those things called grades, which seemed to be the only way to determine her worth in life. Instead of just doing a project to get it done, she took on everything like she was working toward a Nobel Peace Prize: "I believe how you do one thing in life is how you do everything! So drop in big!"

HAVE CAMERA, WILL TRAVEL

On graduation, Alison set off with camera and surfboard to translate all she had seen and learned, and wanted to experience moving forward into moving film documents, which instantly garnered attention and awards.

Alison's first project, a short film called *Rita*, was about her first indoor school experience, in the high Himalayas. It won international acclaim at numerous film festivals, including Telluride. She won Telluride again the next year with her Moroccan surf adventure film *Snaked!*, the cobra-kissing surfing adventure that she wrote, produced, directed, shot, edited, and starred in.

INCANTATIONS

At 23 years old, Alison completed her first feature-length documentary, *INCANtations*, which earned her international recognition after premiering at Patagonia's Wild and Scenic Film Festival. She was recently named one of the top twenty-five college filmmakers by MTV, and *Rita* was nominated for an MTV movie award in 2007. In 2008 she teamed up with world-class athletes as the star surfer in the film *Nature Propelled*, narrated by Patrick Stewart. Then she was a finalist for Steven Spielberg and Mark Burnett's show "On the Lot."

2009: EAT PRAY LOVE

In 2009 Alison was honored by Meryl Streep for being one of the top emerging female artists. She was also excited to work on the Hollywood blockbuster *Eat Pray Love* because Ketut Liyer, the Balinese medicine man in the film, was her painting teacher while she was growing up in Bali, and miraculously, much of the movie was filmed in the same house in the same village in Bali where she had spent many of her happy childhood years.

2013: NAKED AND AFRAID

Naked and Afraid was Discovery Channel's highest rated series of 2013, and the most-watched show in the network's history. Alison's brilliantly effective appearance on that show took her halfway around the world to the Maldives. "On that Island From Hell," she wrote, "I survived for twenty-one days *and* earned the highest PSR (Primitive Survival Rating) of season one of the series."

Alison traveling by boat
Photo: Lucia Griggi

2013: CLEANING UP THE MALDIVES

During Alison's 21-day survival challenge on that one tiny island in the Maldives, she was shocked by the amount of plastic trash covering it. "It was only one island," Alison said, "and I couldn't bear to imagine what the other 1,200 islands looked like, covered in their own veil of plastic debris."

To leave the island at the end of those harrowing 21 days, Alison and her long-suffering partner in survival, a strapping and courageous Army combat veteran laid low by punishing sunburn, made a raft out of castaway plastic bottles. As they paddled out to their rescue boat, she swore she would return to do something to alert the world to the plague of ocean-borne plastic pollution. Her mission: to rid the world of plastic detritus, and transform the existing plastic waste into usable items. Much of the plastic trash is carried to the island chain from faraway countries by ocean currents, and as it travels it breaks down and pollutes the ocean with toxins that are eaten by fish, and eventually by us. "The Maldives are home to one of the largest tuna fisheries in the world. Isn't it wildly unsettling to think that the next time you take a bite of tuna it could be laden with microscopic, toxic plastic particles?"

Alison returned to the Maldivian island where she survived *Naked and Afraid* to document the isolated "trash island" and create a comedic short about this serious global issue. The film shares her passion for storytelling and education through entertainment. "The #1 most important thing to pack on any adventure or survival mission is humor! As my wild parental units taught me, the way to inspire positive change is to be positive. . . . Growing up global, the world was my classroom and the ocean my playground—I hope to keep it plastic free and friendly for future generations to explore, learn from, and love!"

2013+: ALISON'S ADVENTURES

And now, like a female version of Indiana Jones—always with a camera and a pink surfboard—Alison journeys into ancient cultures to share global secrets of survival, sustainability, and happiness through a unique style of storytelling guided by her voiceover and the wild characters she has met along the way. Her film series *Alison's Adventures* calls attention to global, environmental, and human issues that educate and inspire viewers to be part of the solution. "Each film entertains while teaching cultural awareness, geographic exploration, and the importance of family, kindness, health, and caring for our planet."

Alison's view from beneath
Photo: Lucia Griggi

So far, *Alison's Adventures* have led her to Fiji, New Zealand, Switzerland, and even close to her Hawaiian home.

VOLCANO SURF ADVENTURE

In fact, Alison's most recent film adventure happened close to the Big Island of Hawaii. Kilauea Volcano's eruption was flowing into the sea for the first time in many years when Alison was invited to paddle within feet of the hot steaming lava, and this became a Discovery Channel episode. Since she was a little girl, Alison has always felt a connection with the earth, or the *aina*, as Hawaiians call it, and its continuous creation. Her lifelong dream was to paddle her pink surfboard into a volcanic area to feel a true connection to earth as it is being formed by the superheated primordial force of lava boiling into the steaming sea mist. That dream came true. "With the guidance, support, and prayer of the elders, and following cultural protocol," Alison wrote. "I paddled within feet of hot lava waterfalls pouring into the ocean. It was humbling and breathtaking. The rawness, the heat, the crackling and hissing sounds, the reality check that we live on a planet that is alive, and growing, its tumultuous growing pains, the hiss and crackle of flowing lava and the smell of earth's furnace. This taught me that life is beautiful, short, and fragile, and not worth stressing about because all that we know and can know is always in a state of flux. We can own nothing but our memories, and if we can love unselfishly they will sustain us—and the earth if we protect it."

ALISON'S NEXT ADVENTURE

What's next for Alison Teal? Alison is putting the final editing touches on her latest film that is perhaps the most dangerous and daring quest of her life. She slipped into a sealskin-thick wetsuit to brave the dark, chilly, Pacific Northwest waters of British Columbia and teamed up with a local wild woman, Nikki, who spent 18 months surviving on the coast of BC in a row boat with little but a feral cat. Together they braved a new adventure for Alison—becoming one with the great grizzly bear. The *Alison's Adventures: British Columbia* film is launching soon on her website so stay tuned!

Beauty: Sally and the boat are both smiling as she checks out the surf at Tavarua, Fiji.
Photo: Lucia Griggi

And the Beast: Sally on a big, blustery day at Margaret River in Western Australia. She likes the power.
Photo: Lucia Griggi

Born: December 19, 1990
Birthplace: Gerroa, New South Wales, Australia

THE PEOPLE'S CHAMPION

As an athlete you have to show determination and diligence; no one else is going to get you up at 4:30 a.m. to train by yourself. I have that work ethic ingrained in me, and I think it's put me in a great position to launch a business career.

—*Sally Fitzgibbons*

I think Sal is a one-off. She has a great athletic mind—her background was in middle distance running—and she has really applied it to figuring out how to be the best surfer she can be. She has had a lot of help from her dad, Martin, who has clearly encouraged her to see beyond the surf industry loop. She's a strong character, very determined, puts a lot on the line, yet there is nothing abrasive about her—you'd search far and wide to find anyone who'd have a bad word to say about her. She doesn't play cute, though a lot of people think she is, which is another mark of her character and athletic mind; it must be a big temptation for a girl to play to the male gaze, but Sal never goes there. She is a lot of fun to surf with; the sense is always that she is really enjoying that time in the water, and she doesn't blow waves.

—*Nick Carroll, noted Australian surfer and writer*

SURF OR TURF?

In 2007, the Fitzgibbons family gathered 'round the kitchen table at their home in Gerroa, New South Wales, and made a fateful decision: Sally Fitzgibbons was a

17-year-old athlete who was excelling by land and sea. As a runner, Sally had won gold medals in the 800 metre and 1500 metre races at the Australian Olympic Festival—an international, multi-sport event held in January of 2007 for athletes from 13 to 19 years old.

The for-real Olympics were maybe somewhere off in the future, but more immediately, there was a spot for Sally in the World Youth Track and Field Championships in the Czech Republic. Sally had the paces. She qualified.

But Sally was having even greater success as an amateur surfer.

What began for fun at eight years old in the surf around Gerroa was getting serious for Sally, eight years later. In 2006 she finished runner up at the 2006 ISA World Junior U16 Surfing Championships in Brazil. In May of 2007, Sally won the ISA World Junior U18 Championship at Costa da Caparica in Portugal. From there, Fitzgibbons found her pace and went on a holy tear. Competing at the US Open in Huntington Beach, Fitzgibbons shook up the world when she rung up four of the top 10 wave scores, made the semifinals and finished third—at 16

Sally boldly going where few women are keen to go: getting towed into a Sydney slab called Ours.
Photo courtesy Martin Fitzgibbons/Fitzgibbons International

years old: "A third at the US Open at my first trip to Huntington isn't too bad," Fitzgibbons understated to Chris Roots of *The Illawarra Mercury*.

In September of 2007 she won the Billabong Pro Junior in Wollongong and then won the Australian Junior series title at Bells Beach a month later.

AMAZING

In October of 2007, Sally competed at the Beachley Classic World Tour event at Queenscliff Beach in Sydney. In the opening round, she rudely beat one of her inspirations and idols, the seven-time Australian world champion for whom the contest was named—Layne Beachley.

Beachley got the upstart back in a later round.

In 2007 Sally also won the Billabong World Junior U21 Championship at North Narrabeen to claim her second amateur world title. "My 2007 was amazing," she told Chris Roots. "I have two world titles to my name, and I never dreamed of getting those so quickly. I just had goals and set out to do anything to achieve them."

SHIN SPLINTS OR SURF TRIPS?

A fork in the road. A meeting at the kitchen table with her father, Martin, and mother, Mary. A life decision to be made: running or surfing?

Shin splints or surf trips?

Sore thighs or the Mentawais?

"I love surfing, and it wasn't really that hard to make a decision," Fitzgibbons said to Chris Roots.

TEN YEARS AFTER

Ten years after, looking back on that decision in the fullness of time, it has all panned out nicely. Competing as a pro from 2009 to 2015, Sally won nine WSL World Tour events—including two prized bell trophies from the Bells Beach events; two wins at Tavarua, Fiji; a victory in Brazil; and a US Open. In almost a decade of professional surfing, Sally has won close to a million dollars in prize money and likely earned multiples of that from her sponsors. And then she left her major sponsors and tried her entrepreneurial skills at building her own brand, Fitzgibbons International. She has written a best-selling book and inspired Australians and people around the world to live an active, healthy life—to live their passions.

Sally has seen the world, partied with rock stars, and gotten heaps of waves. But in all that, there is one distinction that has eluded her: a professional surfing world championship. She has finished runner-up multiple times and been in the top five since she debuted in 2009 but has been unable to get past the twin towers of Carissa Moore and Stephanie Gilmore.

Does that bug her? Sally is known for being smiley, but behind that smile there are gritted teeth. She is only 26, super-fit, and determined. Will 2016 be her year to bring a professional surfing championship title back to Gerroa?

ROOTS

Sally Fitzgibbons comes from a family of competitors in a nation of competitors. She was born and grew up in the small town of Gerroa, on the south coast of New South Wales, about 60 miles south of Sydney, surrounded on one side by the raw natural beauty of southeast Australia and on the other by the deep blue sea. It offers surfing, snorkeling, fishing, and great places for coastal runs.

How small a town is Gerroa? "The sign says population 500," Sally said, "but that is in the holidays, so more like 200 regulars."

Sally was the youngest of four children—the rest were boys, all surfers—born to Mary and Martin, both teachers who lived the majority of their married lives in Gerroa. "Dad is a surfer but not Mum," Sally said. "They were both quite sporty, and Mum would have a go at most things."

Growing up in the country, within a sporting family, Sally also had a go at many things. She and her brothers played similar sports. In Gerringong, a slightly larger town not too far away, she played soccer, touch football, and hockey and did surf lifesaving training.

A bit unusual for a surfer, Sally also was a runner. She was the Australian national champion in the 800 and 1,500 meters and won gold medals in those events at the Youth Olympics in 2007. She also made state teams for soccer and touch football.

Jock! Gerringong is far enough south for winters to be cold, so for Sally and her mates, it was traditional sports in winter and ocean sports in summer. She rode waves on a body board until the age of 5, and then Dad started pushing her into waves. "I took to it pretty quickly and loved surfing with Dad," she said.

SOUTH COAST OF NEW SOUTH WALES

As Google Earth flies, the south coast of New South Wales covers about 240 miles from Sydney to the Victoria border. But the coastline is many more miles of nooks, crannies, beaches, headlands, points, reefs, surf, surf, surf, and surfers, surfers, surfers—some of them world-class competitors. "The south coast has produced a few World Tour surfers past and present," Sally said: "Kai Otton, Mick Lowe, Todd Prestage, Tyler Wright, Owen Wright, Anthony MacDonald, and Pam Burridge, so we are well represented from this region."

Sally represented the region well in the traditional sports, and she began competitive surfing at age 11 at the Rusty Gromfest. She continued competing up and down the east coast in grom events, eventually breaking into the pro ranks at age 17.

Runner Cathy Freeman, who won gold at the 2000 Sydney Olympics, inspired Sally, and surfers Layne Beachley and Kelly Slater were in their prime when she was growing up.

All her success as a runner translated well into surfing as Sally began to light up the world of amateur surfing beginning in 2004 at age 14. She was the youngest surfer to win the ASP Pro Junior, open to anyone under the age of 21. Sally was 14 when she won the event, held on Queensland's Sunshine Coast.

On the same day, Sally also finished second at the Billabong Easter Girls Festival, a professional World Qualifying Series event. There was more to come.

She won the Australasian Pro Junior Series in 2007 and 2008 and at age 16 represented Australia at the International Surfing Association U18 World Titles in Brazil, placing second. When she was 16, Fitzgibbons won her first championship at the ISA U18 World Titles in Portugal. The next year she won the Billabong ASP U21 World Title and the ISA World Games Open Title.

ATHLETIC

In *The Encyclopedia of Surfing*, Matt Warshaw described Sally Fitzgibbons as an "Athletic regular foot pro surfer from New South Wales, Australia. . . . By 2010, Fitzgibbons was among the favorites at each tour event, and she finished the year ranked second, behind reigning world champion Stephanie Gilmore. She went on to win the Rip Curl Pro Bells Beach in 2011, claiming runner-up at season's end to Carissa Moore, and then won the Rip Curl Pro again in 2012, defeating Gilmore in the final."

Warshaw says of Fitzgibbons that she "prefers a clean and wholesome approach; she doesn't drink, is friendly in media interviews, and is a prolific social media user, cheerfully Tweeting support for her favorite Aussie pro sports teams. In 2012 and 2015, she was named Female Surfer of the Year at the Australian Surfing Awards."

Eye of the tigress. Sally Fitzgibbons crunching her abs, in anticipation of late drops and gouging cutbacks to come.
Photo courtesy Martin Fitzgibbons/Fitzgibbons International

SHE'S GOT THE LOT

Two video clips are linked from Sally's write-up in the *Encyclopedia*, and to watch them is to agree with Warshaw's "athletic" tag. Sally Fitzgibbons has got legs. Her style has been cleansed of any hesitations or glitches or half turns. She loves to thwack the lip hard, frontside or backside, and you can evidence those champion legs in how hard she turns and how she completes her turns.

Sally must have grown up with a left point in the 'hood, because her backside turns are fulsome and satisfying: hard off the bottom, straight up into the lip, and always moving forward. There's a bit of Kelly Slater in her style, especially backside (and she smiled to herself when she read that).

From Bells Beach to some random wave pool in Abu Dhabi, Sally combines classic, solid, power surfing style with a bag of thoroughly modern tricks: tail slides, 360s, aerials.

She's got the lot: Championship speed, style, aggression, and attitude, and those qualities have propelled her to the top.

GOING PRO

In 2008 professional surfing was administered by the Association of Surfing Professionals, and both the men's and women's tours had a two-tier system. To qualify for the World Championship Tour, surfers had to perform on the grueling World Qualifying Series: fourteen events rated from One Star to Six Star, beginning in Australia in January and finishing in Hawaii in December. Sally Fitzgibbons won the first two events in Australia and qualified for the WCT in the first five events—setting a record to become the youngest WQS-to-WCT qualifier in ASP history.

The girl was on fire.

Sally started the 2009 WCT Tour with a bullet. She won a WQS event in Portugal, didn't win a Championship Tour event, but finished fifth overall, after suffering a back injury at the first event, for the Championship Tour at the end of the year.

> "I love surfing, and it wasn't really that hard to make a decision."

RING THE BELL(S)

In 2010 Sally spent the season dueling with Steph Gilmore. They met in three finals; Gilmore won all three, and Fitzgibbons finished the season runner-up to that Gilmore girl.

She won her first ASP WCT event in April 2011 at Bells Beach, a long, powerful, varietal reef/point break that is perfectly suited for Sally's athletic style. "This is so overwhelming," she told Justin Cote for Grind TV.

It's been a long journey for me to finally win, and this is incredible. I can't feel my arms or legs, and I'm just trying to keep from crying right now. It's been a really long time coming, and I want to thank all the girls for pushing me, as well as all my family and friends who have supported me over the years.

Winners of the Rip Curl Pro at Bells Beach, Australia, get to ring the bell. Sally has rung it twice. She likes the way it sounds—like victory!
Photo courtesy of Fitzgibbons International

It's extra special to win it this year for the fifty-year event. Ever since I was a kid, I've always watched my heroes surf and win here, and I've always dreamed of ringing the bell; and now that it's happened, I don't know what to say. The other night at the fifty-year ball, I saw all my icons on stage and I was so inspired. So to win right now is a dream come true.

Sally beat Carissa Moore in the final of the Subaru Pro in New Zealand in April, claiming the world #1 ranking, then beat Lakey Peterson in the final of the US Open of Surf in California—in front of God, the surf media, the surf industry, and everyone.

She finished runner-up to Carissa Moore for the 2011 championship.

POPULAR

Sally made an impression on surf fans in California and around the world as she finished fifth in 2011 and second in the 2013, 2014, and 2015 Surfer Poll Awards. Then she was awarded three times at the 2012 ASP World Surfing Awards. First

From the east coast of Australia to the east coast of Canada—Sally throwing a lovely rooster tail of spray somewhere in the myriad nooks and crannies of Nova Scotia
Photo courtesy of Martin Fitzgibbons

was for being runner-up in the 2011 World Tour. The second award she shared with Carissa Moore for winning the Women's ASP Heat of the Year, and she was honored with the ASP Surfers' Surfer award, which was voted on by her peers.

In February 2012 Sally Fitzgibbons was competing at the Roxy Pro in Queensland, Australia. Janna Irons asked her how much she wanted to win the world title. "Hmm . . . on a scale of 1 to 10, I would say about a 10+. It's always the goal when you start the year, but it always seems so far away. But I'm definitely ready and strong, confident and comfortable where I am at the moment, so we'll see how it unfolds." What unfolded was that Sally won Bells again, and also the contest in Rio de Janeiro, but finished runner-up for the world title—again—to that Gilmore girl.

MOORE-GILMORE

Carissa Moore won the world title in 2013. Steph Gilmore won it in 2014.

In 2015 the ASP World Tour became the World Surf League World Tour. Carissa Moore won the first year of the WSL Championship Tour. Meanwhile, Sally proved her grit in the surf at Cloudbreak, on the Fijian island of Tavarua, in the kind of surf where she excels.

PERSEVERANCE

Sally Fitzgibbons was the defending champion at the 2015 Fiji Pro, and she was keen to defend that title. All was going smoothly until her round-two heat against Mahina Maeda. Fitzgibbons pulled into the barrel on a well-overhead wave and fell, then fell a couple other times, but true to Greg Noll's wipeout philosophy: "It's never the one you think it's gonna be, kid." At the end of one of her waves, Sally fell in a seemingly harmless way, but she got injured.

The WSL webcast replay shows Sally holding her left ear and Maeda paddling up, asking what's wrong, and waving for the ski to come and get Sally. She was paddling with one arm and holding her ear with the other.

Fortunately the heat was over, and Sally had enough points to advance to round three. Doctors examined her and told the Australian she had perforated her eardrum: "It was like someone had poked a hole through my ear," she said.

Always a smile as she takes
down another win
Photos: Lucia Griggi

Doctors advised her not to compete. "I had put so much into my preparation for the event, turning up a week early and surfing double to triple overhead waves," Sally said. "I just wasn't ready to give up."

Round three was to run shortly after, on the afternoon of her injury. There was long debate from officials whether Sally should continue. After hearing all the facts, she decided to push on and compete in round three in slightly smaller, windier surf. The punctured eardrum didn't seem to affect her performance, as she defeated Laura Enever and Lakey Peterson.

Winning round three meant Sally didn't have to surf in round four. She defeated Laura Enever in the quarterfinal, then Lakey Peterson in the semifinal.

The final was held in meaty, challenging, double-overhead surf, and Sally beat South African goofy foot Bianca Buitendag to defend her title—and cement her legend, with the judges claiming it was the best women's surfing they had seen.

Surfing with a punctured eardrum is no fun, and more wipeouts could have led to more extreme pain and further damage. But Sally is a competitor.

FIRST COMES LOVE, THEN COMES MARRIAGE

In 2015 Sally published the book *Live Like Sally*; the Train Like Sally app was released in 2016: "My initial download of the fitness knowledge I've learned over years of being an athlete," she wrote on her website. "I've learned so much about building a holistically strong body with a huge variety of fitness forms, whether it's boxing, HIIT, swimming, gym sessions, or body weight exercises. Training should be fun; it shouldn't be a chore, and the secret to sticking to your programs is variety. TLS can be for an exercise first-timer, all the way through to those wanting to push the limits and be their very best athlete."

She also said "Yes." According to her website, "2015 was a milestone year for Sally, not just as a businesswoman and athlete but also in her personal life. Now fiancé Trent Merrin—National Rugby League star and also dedicated athlete—and Sally were engaged in November during a romantic Vanuatu getaway."

While living in a Gerroa dream on the south coast of New South Wales, Sally remains dedicated to her vision. "I want to help people realize, 'You know what, I can do anything I put my mind to.' There's nothing ever wrong or embarrassing about trying your very best."

Sally's training pays off
Photo: Lucia Griggi

TEN YEARS AFTER

Almost ten years after Sally Fitzgibbons sat down at the kitchen table with her parents and chose surf over turf, she has seen the world from Gerroa and back again, partied with rock stars, witnessed a street shooting in Rio de Janeiro, won events, lost events, almost won the world title many times, and got a hole in her ear that hurt like hell—and went on to win the contest anyway.

Sally has had a blast, fallen in love, built a home, written a book, launched a business, started a charity foundation, and fulfilled dreams she didn't even know she had. But there is one goal that has remained elusive: a professional world surfing title. Sally is competitive and goal driven; you know it has to bother her that she hasn't won the title yet. Doesn't it?

Sally's father, Martin, commented on his daughter—all she had accomplished and was yet to accomplish and what she was about:

> While Sal hasn't won a world title—and yes that ambition is 100 percent still there—the individuality and uniqueness of Sally comes from what happens outside of a jersey. No other surfer has ever tried to build a business, launch a foundation, write a book, and cross over into mainstream media (beyond surf) while they're still competing on tour as one of the best and most feared surfers. [Sally has made the final of 40 percent of all events since being on tour in 2009.]
>
> Sally is looking into the NOW, and because of her ambitious, larger-than-life hardwiring, she took on the challenge, walked away from the biggest female surf sponsors, Roxy and also Red Bull, to write her own history, build her own brand and legacy, and reinvent the way women are seen not just in the surfing world, not just in the fitness world, but also in the business world by learning to be a young entrepreneur. Winning a world title has little to do with Steph and Carissa, who Sally is friends with. She wishes them all the best and celebrates their achievements. Winning a world title is all about your own personal journey of becoming the best surfer you can be in any given year.

Founded in 2015, Fitzgibbons International has several employees that provide marketing services to companies like Samsung, Canon, Novotel, Land Rover, and other partners while also building products like the Train Like Sally fitness app. In November 2016 Sally hosted her own World Surf League Q6000 surf event at the Sydney International Beach Festival, which was also a celebration of Sally's brand of living an active lifestyle. The event included ocean swims, a 12k fun run, world record fitness attempts, and a chance to learn to surf with the pros.

Sally's charity foundation, DREAM, uses the mantra "DRop Everything And Move," which looks to develop DREAM squads everywhere and is now working with the New South Wales government to help activate children in the school system on a large scale. She aims to take this program to Tour stops around the world. "Sally basically wants to help people make active, healthy choices," Martin said.

Sally is always looking to elevate her surfing outside the Tour to stay connected to her core roots of surf, that is, exploring and looking for surf in unique locations that will test her skill level. Sally just last month surfed a wave that's been rarely tackled by women, Cape Fear (Ours). She spent hours at a UAE Wadi wave pool, pushing the performance levels of her sport, learning to do and performing hundreds of air-reverses, and busting down every stereotype of women's surfing with gritty performances like Fiji. Sally is a people's champion. Fans love and connect with how hard she tries and how hard the losses hurt and how much she loves life.

And isn't that what it's all about in the end—love? Gotta love what you do, and that shines in everything Sally Fitzgibbons has accomplished.

The voice of professional surfing, we welcome you, Rosy Hodge.
Photo: Lucia Griggi

Born: April 27, 1987
Birthplace: East London, South Africa

THE FACE, THE VOICE

I loved the traveling and the surfing, but it was s-o-o-o disappointing to lose. I feel like I didn't have enough confidence in myself and I would make silly mistakes. I sometimes wish I could take what I know now and apply it to my years on tour. But I'm really happy to be where I am now and doing this job.

—*Rosy Hodge*

THE SWELLOQUENT VOICE OF PROFESSIONAL SURFING

Rosy Hodge has never been to Pedro's Tacos in her new hometown of San Clemente (nor the Pedro's Tacos in Fallbrook or Oceanside), but she's been just about everywhere else. Originally from South Africa, where she dodged white sharks and had a promising amateur career, Rosy traveled the world as a professional surfer for four years then picked up a microphone, stood in front of a camera, and liked how it felt. Now she is one of the faces and voices of the World Surf League webcasts, which broadcasts professional surfing to the world in a professional way.

As a color commentator, Rosy is colorful. Rosy is tall. Rosy is blond. Rosy is pretty. Rosy is, well, rosy! She's sunny, and she speaks with that South African accent, precision. and elocution that make Prince William sound like a chimney sweep.

She is very good on camera. She clearly loves her job. And as a former pro who has seen the world, she speaks from experience—making her the best kind of commentator.

DEREK TAKES A STAB AT ROSY

Derek Reilly is the editor of stabmagazine.com—an Internet site straight outta Australia that is not afraid to push the boundaries. In Stab issue #65 Reilly got pretty excited while drinking "plonk" (cheap Australian alcohol) with South African surfer/model/online commentator Rosy Hodge—All 5'10" and 148 pounds of her:

Oh, aren't our prayers answered! Here, pictured, we see the marvelous Rosy Hodge, a pro surfer of course, sponsored all the way to the hilt by Roxy, but who is also the undisputed queen of the post-heat interview. A world champion of the post-heat interview, if awards were awarded for such things.

Don't you even dare tell me you're unaware of her broad South African vowels and hair that flashes like warped gold or of the way she towers over her subjects, projecting a comely blend of intimidation and sex appeal.

Often, and now that I've mentioned it, you'll notice it; big names, household names, stare wide-eyed with their very famous mouths fixed open.

"Ah, can you repeat the question?"

Beautiful inside and out
Photo: Lucia Griggi

A TALL DRINK OF WATERWOMAN

Reilly was turning the tables here, throwing questions at a young woman who has become the female voice and face of the World Surf League webcasts. Hodge works alongside Peter Mel, Strider Wasilewski, Joe Turpel, Ross Williams, Martin Potter, Todd Kline, and Ronnie Blakey to report on contest action by land, sea, and air, thrusting microphones at pro surfers before, during, and after heats.

An active job, an exciting job, a job that keeps Rosy traveling around the world year-round, the Brooke Baldwin of surfing—a tall drink of waterwoman who knows what she is talking about. Rosy Hodge isn't just a beautiful speaking voice; she is also a top professional surfer.

Rosy, behind the scenes, duck-diving at Backdoor
Photo: Lucia Griggi

ROOTS

Rosy is originally from East London, South Africa, a small coastal town along a wild coast equally blessed/cursed with incredibly long right points and incredibly dangerous white sharks. She was mentored by the likes of four-time Women's World Champion Wendy Botha and local pros Greg Emslie and Royden Bryson.

Rosy came from a water family. Her dad pushed her into her first wave at Nahoon beach break in the summer of 1994 on an MR twin. She was totally hooked because she loved the feeling of gliding on the water. Her mom doesn't like getting her face wet and is scared of the ocean, but she drove Rosy and her brother to the beach every day and flashed the lights of the car when they needed to come in.

Rosy wanted to keep up with her older brother, who pushed her to do whatever he was doing. "He made me tough. We would go skate and he would say, 'You have to acid drop off this scary ledge or I'm leaving you here.' I would cry but try to do it anyway." About her family she says, "My dad is one of my favorite people; I love surfing or doing anything with him. I'm so fortunate to have a family that supports me so much. My mom will stay up and watch every heat with a cup

Rosy power cutback, Hawaii
Photo: Lucia Griggi

Rosy taking a jump into a waterfall in Puerto Rico
Photo: Lucia Griggi

of rooibos [herbal tea] back home and send me cute messages of encouragement or screenshots of me at the desk."

Rosy was a competitive swimmer and sailor as a girl. A year after she started surfing at age 7, the local Roxy representative saw her and signed her to a contract at 8 years old. When she was 16 Barry Wollins of Roxy SA sent her to Fiji to compete in the wildcard trials at Cloudbreak. He told her if she wanted to surf professionally, she would need to get an international contract and be paid in American dollars.

Rosy was excited, but also intimidated. She had never surfed waves like Cloudbreak. She traveled alone to Fiji. "It's a long way from home, and the girls on tour back then weren't as friendly as they are now." She didn't win the trials, but she surfed an expression session. Photographers took shots of Rosy from a helicopter, and she ended up getting a double-page spread in the international girls' surfing magazines. Roxy sent her to Hawaii at the end of that year. She signed a contract in January and has been part of the family ever since.

South Africa is a country absolutely lashed by great surf from one side to the other, and it has produced a lot of champion surfers, including Shaun and Michael Tomson, Wendy Botha, and Jordan "Jordy" Smith. At 9 years old, Rosy competed in the Boy's Under-10 division. When she was 11 she competed on the Under-19 girls team and traveled to Bali for the ISA World Juniors. "I think I came in ninth," Rosy said.

GOING PRO

Rosy graduated from high school in 2005, and 2006 was her first year on the ASP World Qualifying Series. Rosy needed only one year of competition to qualify for the 2007 ASP Women's World Tour and competed from 2007 to 2011.

She loved the traveling and the surfing, but she hated to lose. "I feel like I didn't have enough confidence in myself and I would make silly mistakes. I sometimes wish I could take what I know now and apply it to my years on tour."

In 2008 Rosy finished ninth in every WCT event she competed in. Her best finish was a second place to Paige Hareb at the Drug Aware Pro Margaret River presented by O'Neill Australia—a WQS event.

In 2009 Rosy took a third at the Rip Curl Search in Portugal and a fifth in the next event at the Movistar Peru Classic, competing against Peruvian champion

Rosy the riveting surf correspondent, on the job at the Quiksilver Pro, France, in 2014. Rosy is grilling Brazilian pro Jadson Andre, who lost in the final to John John Florence. This was before the Association of Surfing Professionals tour became the World Surf League tour.
Photo: Lucia Griggi

Sofía Mulánovich in the final. Rosy finished tenth in the final ratings for 2009—and was voted Most Improved by her peers.

For the 2010 season, Rosy finished ninth in the first seven WCT events, then seventeenth in the final event, and ended the season getting put back on the World Qualifying series.

In 2011 Rosy competed in four WQS events, but her results weren't too great. "I did well at the good waves, like Honolua Bay and Portugal. I wish I had done better on tour seriously; you lose and you just feel like you want another go."

It was time for something else.

ROSY GETS A SECOND ACT

F. Scott Fitzgerald once said, "There are no second acts in American lives." But Rosy isn't American, and she did get a second act, beginning in 2010. Back in Hawaii after being knocked off tour at the end of 2010, she ran into the production manager for the WSL, who was also the product manager for Quik and Roxy with Mark Warren. They invited her to commentate at the Quik/Roxy Pro at Snapper, and Rosy was excited to try it. "First interview I did was with Patty G. I asked him if he was going to do another Rodeo Flip like the one he did in Tahiti, and he politely reminded me that Snapper is a right-hand point."

Oops!

But Rosy got a little less nervous as the competition went on. Rip Curl then asked her if she would like to do Bells. She did and was then asked to do the competition in Western Australia and the Quik Pro in France. After that it was built into her Roxy contract to commentate their events. The ASP is now the WSL, and they approached Rosy to do the full tour in 2013. "I absolutely love my job; I don't ever take it for granted. I haven't done any formal training, but everyone on the WSL gives us a heads-up on how to improve."

Using the miracle of Internet communications, a mass e-mail went out to a wide variety of pro surfers and fellow commentators around the world, essentially asking: "Rosy Hodge. What's she like, then? Is she a good sort?"

Australian journalist Nick Carroll said that Rosy was indeed a good sort: "Rosy's a gem. Good parents. She's really grounded, warm, intelligent, and has grown a lot in the past two and half years of WSL commentary duties. She's obviously very attractive but doesn't play to it, doesn't even seem to notice it, which is a great attribute in anyone in my opinion. Super fun to surf with."

Tara Mel, wife of Peter Mel, a big-wave surfer and fellow commentator on the WSL with Rosy, also likes her:

> I really enjoy any time that I share with Rosy. Watching her blossom into a professional broadcaster has been a great pleasure. She's made me laugh and cry all in one sitting. A very special gal.
>
> Rosy is also very funny. She likes to laugh and can be a little naughty with her jokes. Very witty in private, she cracks me up. Also very respectful to nature and connects with a spiritual and almost superstitious manner: Meaning she has a certain mindfulness to how she interacts and talks about it. Specifically experiences with surfing, but carries over to all

Rosy frolicking on the North Shore of Hawaii
Photo: Lucia Griggi

interactions. Please don't forget to ask about her shark experience at her house where she grew up.

THE SHALLOWS

Okay, what about that shark experience at her house where she grew up? Rosy's reality mirrored the art of the recent movie *The Shallows*. In May 2010 Rosy was surfing north of East London at Queensberry Bay with her friend Greg Emslie. Rosy caught a wave and was paddling back out when she saw Emslie sitting on his board with his feet up, being circled by two large fins. "Then Greg started shouting and I thought, 'Oh, cool, he's claiming my wave,'" Rosy was quoted by

> ## As I got close I saw that it was a giant shark showing its dorsal and tail fins, and I realized that Greg was in serious trouble.

Craig Jarvis. "Earlier in the day we had some dolphins around, and when I saw the two fins I thought there were two dolphins by Greg. As I got close I saw that it was a giant shark showing its dorsal and tail fins, and I realized that Greg was in serious trouble."

Emslie *was* in serious trouble, being circled by a 4-meter white shark—a car with teeth—the man and the shark staring each other down, eyeball to eyeball, seeing who would flinch and who would attack. As Emslie worried about his wife and kids, he saw Rosy approaching. "Greg shouted at me to go in, and I remember saying, 'What about you?' But there wasn't much I could do, so I headed over to the rocks."

As Rosy scrambled up the rocks, she looked back to see a wave approaching. "The shark was watching me so closely," Emslie said. "We were just staring at each other: full on eyeball to eyeball. The shark definitely checked the wave as well and was waiting to see what I was going to do. It was so close, and the situation was so tense. I thought that if I started paddling, it would simply attack. So I waited until the last split second. I did like one stroke, caught the wave, went left and straight over the bricks."

Emslie joined Rosy on the rocks, and it took both of them days to get over the adrenaline of a near-death experience.

THE MICK INCIDENT

Growing up as a surfer in South Africa, the risk of shark attack is always there. So Rosy wasn't as shocked as some when World Champion surfer Mick Fanning had a tussle with a big white shark during a 2015 Championship Tour contest at Jeffrey's Bay in South Africa. Rosy was commentating when Mick was confronted by "the shark seen 'round the world." She was watching the final and doing the post-interviews, and Pete Mel was in the water. She watched it happen live and ran upstairs to watch in the booth. After she interviewed Commissioner Renato Hickel to ask what they would do because the contest was on hold, she then ran to the beach to make sure her boyfriend, Ian, was OK. He had gone to surf the Bone Yards before the final and had been in knee-deep water about to paddle out when the shark incident happened. Rosy was impressed by the way Mick handled the incident, as well as the feeling of community among the athletes. "Everyone closed ranks around Mick and celebrated him being OK and made sure his family knew he was fine. Pretty badass that he came back to win this year [2016]; Mick is a hero."

AROUND THE WORLD AND BACK AGAIN

Rosy is now based in San Clemente, California, close to the surf spots at Trestles and within range of the surf industrial complex of Orange County. Why San Clemente? It can't be because of Pedro's Tacos, because Rosy hasn't eaten there yet.

"It kind of just worked out that way," Rosy said. She had broken up with her boyfriend of seven years, and because she was always traveling, nowhere really felt like home. She ended up in California doing some work with Roxy. After spending time in Manhattan Beach, where the waves were "pretty bad," she

Rosy Hodge throwing all 5'10"
into a top turn at Pupukea
Beach Park, Hawaii
Photo: Lucia Griggi

started hanging out with her boyfriend in San Clemente. She discovered that the waves were better there and found an apartment in 2013—the first place she had ever rented on her own. Now she and her boyfriend own a two-bedroom apartment on the Loop at State Park. "We are stoked. The community here is pretty awesome. I can ride my bike to some quality waves, I can walk to the beach, and it's a lot easier to fly from California almost anywhere in the world than it is to fly from South Africa."

FREQUENT FLYER

Rosy does spend a lot of time flying from California.

For the 2015–2016 World Surf League Championship Tour, Rosy started in Australia in the Northern Hemisphere spring (Australia's autumn) for three events on the Gold Coast in Queensland, Bells Beach in Victoria, and Margaret River in Western Australia. Australia is a big country, and that's a lot of traveling right there. But from the Australian leg, Rosy detoured from Rio de Janeiro in May:

Instead of Brazil, I went from California to the Maldives on a boat trip with Tom Carroll and a Roxy/Quik social media contest winner on the *Ocean Divine* for seven days. I went back to California for three days and straight to Fiji for three weeks of contest; back to California for three days; then to Marseille, France, for five days for a Roxy Fitness Event; back to California for three days; and then to South Africa for the JBay Open.

I also had to pull out of Tahiti last week. My boyfriend had an accident, so I just wanted to stay with him and make sure he is OK before I go anywhere.

WSL was awesome about my pulling out at late notice. We travel so much together, it is good to know that if something happens and we need their support, they are going to come through for us. I also couldn't imagine bailing right now to go across the world and not be here with my boyfriend.

Are you exhausted just reading that? We did the math for you. Assuming she left John Wayne Airport and went from event to event without ever going home, that's 40,700 miles to Durban; then Durban to Orange County to Tahiti to Orange County to Biarritz to Lisbon is about 25,000 miles.

Flying from Lisbon to Orange County to Hawaii and back to Orange County is another 10,800 miles. So all told, Rosy was in the air for 100,000 miles plus just for the 2015–2016 tour.

There are few activities more exhausting and health-deteriorating than sitting on an airplane—especially when you're 5'10" and your legs are two-thirds of you. How does Rosy handle all the travel and airport stress and show up looking rosy for the camera?

While the travel has become pretty routine, Rosy does find it a little bit tedious to spend so much time in transit. On the other hand, she is always on the move to locations she loves and that feel like second homes at this point. It's easier than when she was a traveling pro from South Africa, dealing with the stress of arranging and booking her own travel and accommodations. "We have racked up a lot of miles, so we get to upgrade sometimes, but for the most part we travel economy. We always stay at really awesome places. Compared to places I would have booked myself, it is way better."

Rosy has made a nice transition from pro surfer in front of the microphone to broadcaster behind the microphone, but make no mistake, she is still a core surfer. "Let's not forget that Rosy is an absolute 'surf turkey,'" said fellow WSL commentator Peter Mel. "Anytime she has a chance to get in the water, even if it's just for 10 minutes, she will make it happen. A complete joy to work with. A catalyst to the resin, bonding our commentary team."

ROSY MOJO

Fellow South African and surfing champion Shaun Tomson remembers a big winter day in Ventura County when Rosy showed to him she is a serious surfer. "I pull up at Ventura Point in California—it is as big, cold, and challenging as it gets in Southern California, south of Point Concepcion: solid 10 feet with a howling southeast wind trying to make up its mind whether it's sideshore or onshore and waves stacked up to the horizon." He and Rosy paddled out together while a parking lot full of surfers watched, deciding that they didn't want to chance the waves. Glancing back at Rosy as they paddled, he saw she was "absolutely unflustered, paddling with her serene half smile like she's auditioning for a spot in a reality show: relaxed and beautiful under extreme pressure." She waited "like she's riding 3-foot Malibu, charging the long smokin' walls."

He goes on to point out that while you may know Rosy as the presenter, "What you might not know is her solid surf cred, her ability to take it on in conditions that scare the pants off most guys." In fact, "As much as I like Rosie on the mic, I'd like to see her take in a heat here and there, go up head to head against Carissa, Courtney, and Tyler, especially at Bells, Honolua, or Trestles. C'mon WSL, give her a wildcard: She's got the mojo and style to maybe pull off an upset."

Rosy taking some time out on the land
Photo: Lucia Griggi

TURNING JAPANESE

Rosy Hodge has established herself as the female face and voice of pro surfing, and the world seems to be unanimous in its approval. During summer 2016, as Rosy was zipping around the world and the Olympics were on in Rio, the International Olympic Committee gave a thumbs-up to including surfing in the Olympics for Tokyo in 2020.

Four years from now, Rosy will be even more seasoned behind the microphone and in front of the camera. Who better to explain surfing to the world than this tall drink of waterwoman from South Africa, the one with the swelloquent accent and in-depth knowledge of the sport?

No one better.

She flies like the guys. Rosy off the top in Hawaii.
Photo: Lucia Griggi

That was then, this is now. Then, Janet going big with the hair, sometime in the 1960s, while Sean regards it all with quietude.
Photo courtesy Janet Macpherson

Now, Janet in the quietude of her Malibu home, with her gorgeous mother of pearl–inlaid Renny Yater surfboard.
Photo: Lucia Griggi

JANET MACPHERSON

Born: March 24, 1937
Birthplace: San Francisco, California

SURFISTICATE

MALIBU IS THE PLACE TO BE

Malibu is the place to be for the Fourth of July. The surf is traditionally very good—almost every Fourth. The City of Malibu doesn't put on a fireworks display; they leave it to the billionaires and movie stars like Larry Ellison, Barbara Streisand, and Michael Milken to throw down a quarter of a million dollars in chump change and compete with one another to put on the most lavish displays of world-class, cutting-edge fireworks.

Malibu is the place to be on the Fourth of July, and Janet Macpherson's house is one of the best places to be within Malibu. Her house was built (and rebuilt) on a promontory overlooking Surfrider Beach, Malibu Lagoon, Santa Monica Bay, and, off in the distance, Catalina Island, the Palos Verdes Peninsula, and the South Bay from Torrance up to Los Angeles International Airport (LAX). From the grassy knoll in front of her house, she and her family and guests will be able to see the fireworks display at the Malibu Colony and glimpses of other displays all along the coast—all the way to Santa Monica and Torrance and maybe even Palos Verdes.

The view from Janet's house is spectacular, and the inside is a "surfisticated" museum of artifacts collected during decades of surf and adventure travel: an eye-opening collection of arrowheads and shark's teeth collected by Janet and her equally adventurous Australian husband, Steve Farbus, on their many Baja trips, right up to Chinese statues that guard the sliding glass doors. There is a telescope for checking the surf—and the crowds. After all the perfect waves Janet rode in California in the 50s and 60s, and all the perfect waves Janet and Steve have ridden in seclusion around the world, neither of them is keen to deal with the crowds at Surfrider Beach—to battle scores of people for waves that often aren't worth battling over.

Janet charging Pavones circa 2013, surfing hard into her 70s
Photo courtesy Janet Macpherson

On the third of July, Janet is home with her husband, resting and recuperating after a two-month retreat to Scorpion Bay. Janet has been going to Baja for more than forty years, but this time she had a first: "I stepped on a stingray," Janet said, showing off the scar on her tanned, hardened surfer foot. She felt something squishy, and then it hit her like a lightning bolt. After 2 hours of excruciating pain, the poison came out like Jell-O. "That was the most pain I've ever had, and I had Sean natural childbirth. He's 6'4", so he was a big baby."

Janet is no stranger to nature-based trauma. This Malibu home with the commanding view was nearly destroyed by the Canyon Fire of October 2007, and she lost two other houses to the devastating Las Flores Fire in 1993. Malibu is beautiful and benign and okay—until it isn't—but on this day Malibu is showing its best face: The sun is out, the sky is blue, the winds are light, the surf is good, and Janet can see it all from her kitchen.

Usually she and her Australian husband are alone in the house, soaking up the view and the peace and quiet. But Janet's house is the place to be on the Fourth of July, so she has family coming and going: son Sean; daughter-in-law Rachelle; their two cool-named kids, Max and Dash; other nieces and nephews visiting from Northern California and all over. All of them geared up for a Fourth of July party at the Macpherson–Farbus home. A bit more rattle and hum than usual, but it will be over soon.

SURFISTICATION

Janet Macpherson is what you might call a "surfisticate": educated, sophisticated, prosperous, accomplished, hardworking, well-read, well traveled—but a surfer to the core. Janet has been surfing nonstop since 1955, working to surf and surfing to work, traveling as much as possible and then some, and over the years buying and building comfortable surf shacks at some of the world's best surf spots.

Janet surfs as much as possible in the twenty-first century, so as of 2016 she has been surfing for sixty-one years. She is 79, going on 80 and going strong. She can surf Scorpion Bay for hours, step on a stingray, shake it off, and be back out there the next day. At almost 80 years old!

SON SEAN SURFS

Janet's son, Sean, is also a surfisticate. He is visiting California after a few days in Ibiza with his wife, Rachelle—they left their kids, Dashiell and Maxwell, with Other Grandma. From Ibiza to Malibu but soon back to New York, where Sean and Rachelle are often referred to as a "power couple."

Like his mom, Sean is every inch a surfer. But he's also a hardworking, golden touch hotelier/restaurateur/entrepreneur who changed the style of Los Angeles nightlife in the 1980s, then went east to grow with Manhattan's Meatpacking District, and now is a partner in an empire of sleek, chic boutique hotels and relentlessly popular restaurants: the Jane, Maritime, Bowery, Marlton, Ludlow.

From his Malibu roots, Sean's grasp reaches all the way to the eastern edges of the continent, to the very tip of Long Island, where he bought and refurbished

Often referred to as a "New York Power Couple," hotelier/restaurateur Sean Macpherson and his wife, "webtrepeneur" Rachelle Hruska-Macpherson, step out.
Photo courtesy Hruska-Macpherson, Ohana

The Crow's Nest out at Montauk—a restaurant, hotel, and bungalows close to the surf. During the summer, Crow's Nest is packed. Safe to say, Sean has the golden touch. And a lot of that touch, drive, taste, and surfistication comes from Mom.

I stayed in Waikiki for three months. Rented an apartment with my sister and two other sisters. I learned to surf with the beach boys.

ROOTS

Janet was born March 24, 1937, and grew up in the San Francisco you will see in movies like *The Maltese Falcon* and *Pal Joey*. Like Hawaiian princess Ka'iulani, Janet was "the daughter of a double race." Janet's mother came from a prominent family in Mazatlan, Mexico; Paredes is the family name. Her father, Kenneth, was originally from Canada but started Macpherson Leather Company in Montana—and with his brothers stitched and sewed that business into one of the largest saddle makers on the West Coast. Macpherson Leather is a prosperous California institution going back to the early 1900s.

Janet's father died when she was 12, and she was raised by her mother. Janet swam in high school, loved the beach, and was introduced to surfing by a boyfriend in the middle 1950s—a very fun time to be a surfer in California, when

Janet surfing Malibu circa 1965
Photo courtesy Janet Macpherson

Janet at Malibu in living color, snagging one from the crowd, sometime in the mid-1960s
Photo courtesy Janet Macpherson

waves were plentiful, crowds were minimal, and surfboards were evolving from light balsawood to lighter plastics. The mid-50s were the time of *Gidget*, and Janet was one of the first female surfers on the west coast.

JANET GOES HAWAIIAN

Janet graduated from San Francisco's Convent of the Sacred Heart in 1955, and her graduation present was a summer trip to the Hawaiian Islands—when taking a passenger ship to Oahu was one of the most romantic vacations available on Earth. "We sailed over on the *President Cleveland*," Janet told Jamie Brisick for a profile on Janet and Sean in *The Surfer's Journal.* "I stayed in Waikiki for three months. Rented an apartment with my sister and two other sisters. I learned to surf with the beach boys."

Three months surfing Waikiki with the beach boys put the hook in Janet—big time. Back in California, she bought a balsa board from the Velzy/Jacobs surf shop in Venice, California, during a time when not a lot of women surfed—and boards still weighed 30 pounds.

But Janet put that board through its paces and then some. She enrolled at Santa Barbara City College in 1957 and spent many hours surfing Rincon during a time when she had to beg people to surf with her. They would park along a relatively quiet Pacific Coast Highway and usually have the place to themselves.

A dreamy scenario in this crowded world, when a good day at Rincon today will often have more than 200 surfers competing for waves and parking on the PCH will get you towed and/or arrested. Janet had it pristine: "It was really, really lovely," she told Brisick. "I don't like to look back, but those really were the days."

Janet studied education at Santa Barbara City College and graduated from San Francisco State. She would take surf trips down to Santa Cruz in the 1950s, throw her board off the cliff at Steamer Lane, jump in after it, and surf those cold, beautiful waves with no wet suit, no surf leash. Her companions were often the likes of Gus Gustafson, Jim Foley, Jack O'Neill, and the Van Dyke brothers.

After graduating from San Francisco State with a teaching credential, Janet moved to Laguna Beach in Orange County, where she became part of an influential crew of surfers/engineers/entrepreneurs/playboys that included Philip "Flippy" Hoffman—heir to Hoffman Fabrics who would become one of the cornerstones of the modern surf industry. Renny Yater and Tom Morey were both educated surfboard makers—Morey invented the boogie board in the 1970s. And Grubby Clark cornered the market on polyurethane foam surfboard "blanks," made a fortune, and is now the largest private landowner in Oregon.

It was as good as it sounds. Janet and friends would surf all over Southern California and then ski-bum in Alta in the winter.

MOVING TO MALIBU

Janet moved to Malibu in 1960, a year after the movie *Gidget* came out and when the surfin' sensation was rumbling. Where surfing had been a secret thrill enjoyed by small groups up and down the coast through the 1940s and 1950s, riding waves was now mainstream, and surfers from around the world were mainly streaming into Malibu—the spot made famous by *Gidget*, surf music, and the notorious Frankie Avalon and Annette Funicello "surf" movies made by American International Pictures.

In some ways, Malibu was more crowded and treacherous then—surfers rode big, heavy surfboards and didn't wear surf leashes, so paddling out there was perilous. Janet lived on PCH along the beach. She never used the teaching credential but worked as a secretary transcribing movies.

Malibu is a lovely wave, but surfing it in a crowd can be frustrating and hazardous. That is why a lot of Malibu surfers travel—and Janet was one of them. "I traveled to Mexico, Hawaii," Janet said. "I was the first woman they had ever seen surfing in Peru. At Club Waikiki. Over the years I've been to the Seychelles, Reunion Island, South Africa, Africa, Indonesia, the Galapagos Islands. And I have skied all over Europe."

THE ENDLESS SUMMER

By 1964, Bruce Brown had had enough of the "surf music" and "waxploitation" movies created by Hollywood non-surfers to cash in on the surfin' sensation. Brown had been a surfer and moviemaker going back to the "golden years" of the 1950s, and he, like a lot of surfers, was appalled by how Hollywood was depicting his beloved pastime. In 1964 Brown set out on an around-the-world surfing safari with two talented surfers: Mike Hynson and Robert August. Their goal was to show the civilian world what real surfers were like, and to explain to the world that "real surfers don't break into song in front of their girlfriends," as they did in movies like *Gidget* and the Frankie and Annette beach party movies. And Elvis Presley in *Blue Hawaii*, singing "Can't Help Falling in Love" to his girlfriend's granny.

The Endless Summer was a big sensation that swept the nation and became the most successful documentary of any kind up to that point.

TIM MURDOCH

One of the surfers in the New Zealand section of *The Endless Summer* was a local rogue named Tim Murdoch. Janet met Tim in California through surfer Bob Cooper. They married, and Janet moved to New Zealand. She became the New Zealand women's surfing champion and was chosen to represent New Zealand at

Janet among a group of Kiwi surfers, circa 1966. From left: Jonette (Jonnie) Mead, Cyndy Margaret Webb, Pauline Thompson, Gail Pattie, Janet at the back, and Joan Pattie. *Photo courtesy Janet Macpherson and Jonette Mead*

the 1966 World Surfing Championships in San Diego. But she took sick and wasn't all that interested in competition anyway.

Janet also lost interest in both her marriage and New Zealand. She returned to California with a little boy named Sean, her son with Murdoch. Janet doesn't like talking about all that too much, but she did say, "Sean had a lot of dads."

REAL ESTATE TYCOON

By the 1970s, Janet was back in Malibu and showing her own business acumen. She got into real estate, which is how a great many fortunes have been made in Malibu. "I took classes and off I went," Janet told Jamie Brisick, "by the seat of my pants. It was a way to keep the surfing lifestyle. I manage my own properties—all here in Malibu."

Janet now owns several homes around Malibu, which she rents out and uses as a foundation for her surf-travel lifestyle. Any house bought in the 1970s or 1980s is now worth multiples of the original purchase price, as Malibu has evolved from a small, quiet country town into one of the most desirable and expensive places to live in California, the United States, and the world.

HOTEL TYCOON

As Janet became a real estate tycoon, Sean began his path to becoming a hotel tycoon by going to school at Santa Monica High—when Janet would let him. "On good days I had to beg Mom to take me to school," Sean told Brisick.

Mom put the travel bug into Sean, taking long surf trips to Baja and elsewhere beginning when Sean was 14, but always keeping Sean on the education path. "Sean's always been a super-achiever," Janet explained to Brisick. "I never once had to say, 'Do your homework.' His nickname was Dick Tracy because he'd be in the back, taking it all in."

Sean's rise as an entrepreneur is detailed and elaborate and can be found by Googling "Sean Macpherson hotel." He studied business and philosophy at USC and passed through USC's Entrepreneur Program, graduating magna cum laude. Then he threw himself into the world of Los Angeles nightlife in the 1980s: clubs Power Tools to Funky Reggae to Botswana. And then Sean saw the light: Please yourself and hopefully you will please others. "This changed my whole career because I got so much joy out of doing a place that was purely for myself," Sean said to Brisick. "It was basically like a party at my house. Doing that was so rewarding that I saw the light—I had to do projects that I believed in. It changed the way I saw everything."

Out of the 1980s and into the 1990s, the projects Sean believed in included LA clubs El Dorado, Good Luck Bar, Jones, Swingers, El Carmen, and Bar Marmont. Sean's evolutionary point was The Olive, opened in 1991 with no phone number, no signage, nothing external but lots going on inside. Future star Mark Ruffalo was the doorman, letting in the likes of Madonna, Mick Jagger, Robert De Niro, George Clooney, Jack Nicholson, and Kurt Cobain—who almost got into a fist-fight with "Weird Al" Yankovic over his spoof of "Smells Like Teen Spirit."

Sean did this all from the ground up. "I never gave him a penny because he never asked me for a penny," Janet said. "I would have if he had asked, but he never did. I thought what Sean was doing was great. I encouraged him to be an entrepreneur. That's what life is all about. It takes self-confidence to be able to do that."

SEAN TAKES MANHATTAN

Looking for new challenges, Sean began his takeover of New York City in 2001, partnering with Eric Goode on The Park restaurant in 2001, as Manhattan's Meat Packing District was evolving from dangerous to de rigueur. Goode and Macpherson then invested tens of millions of dollars to convert the National Maritime Union Building—a merchant-marine school with tiny, round windows and tinier rooms—into The Maritime, which opened in 2003 with 124 rooms on twelve floors and stands as one of the most popular boutique hotels in New York and the world. "It was not my intent to go into business per se," Sean said to *Haute Living*. "But as my projects continued to work, I became more interested in opening a hotel. The Maritime came up for sale, and I became emotionally connected to the building. A lot of people responded [favorably] to that architecture too, but there were many who thought it was an eyesore."

Sean is so low key, he doesn't even have a Wikipedia page. But Google his name and it will be connected to a mini-empire of NYC institutions.

MOTHER LIKES BEST

Of all Sean's places, The Bowery is the hotel Mom likes best. It's where she always stays, along with all the movie stars. "One time I was riding down in the elevator with a funny black woman—the really pretty one who is a little heavy. We were laughing and joking and when I got out of the elevator the maître d' said 'What were you talking about with . . . ????'" (At Fourth of July, Janet couldn't remember the zaftig actress's name, but the consensus was it was Queen Latifah.)

As for restaurants, Janet likes The Waverly: "You've got to know someone to get in," Janet says. "I like different things, but the $150 macaroni and cheese is a treat."

Through the 80s and 90s and into the twenty-first century, it was work, work, work for Sean Macpherson, but Janet made sure he took time out for surf time.

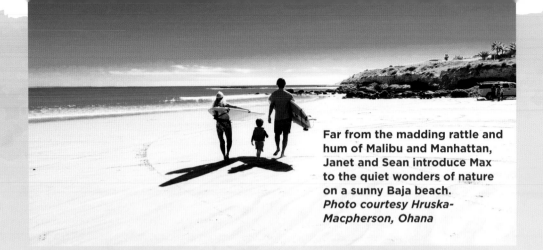

Far from the madding rattle and hum of Malibu and Manhattan, Janet and Sean introduce Max to the quiet wonders of nature on a sunny Baja beach.
Photo courtesy Hruska-Macpherson, Ohana

WORK TO SURF

Janet bought a house in Pavones, Costa Rica, in 1996 and another in Scorpion Bay, Mexico, in 2002. Pavones is a left point break. A long one. Scorpion Bay is a right point break, an even longer one. These are two of the best surf spots in all of the Pacific Coast, and Sean would join Mom a couple of times a year, sometimes bringing down random movie stars like Gina Gershon and Darryl Hannah.

Sean married internet entrepreneur Rachelle Hruska (guestofaguest.com) in summer 2011; they now have two children, Maxwell and Dashiell.

So now Janet's migratory pattern isn't all Pacific Coast and often includes zags to New York City or Aspen to see Sean and Rachelle and her two grandchildren.

SURFAGENARIAN

Janet was born in 1937, so she is now about to turn 80. At an age where many are bedridden like Charlie Bucket's grandparents in *Willy Wonka and the Chocolate Factory*, Janet is surfing, surfing well, and using all that water time to keep herself healthy, vital, moving, and enjoying life.

She can shake shake shake off a stingray sting and go back in the water the next day. That's rad.

Go find a surfer in his or her 70s and 80s and you're likely to see a curious lack of debilitating brain diseases like Alzheimer's and Parkinson's. Janet is sharp as a marble, and that might have something to do with the fact she has lived a healthy, vital life and has doused her brain in adrenalin and endorphins going back to the 1950s.

Janet hanging with Maxwell and Dash and Janet's poodle, fall 2016.
Photo courtesy Hruska-Macpherson, Ohana

HERE TODAY, GONE TO MEXICO

It is the third of July, and Janet Macpherson's house is the place to be. There are barking dogs and shrieking kids and a lot of people going in and out, but that is unusual. On the fourth Janet will throw a party for about twenty friends and family, and then it will be back to peace and quiet. Sean and Rachelle have invited her to the south of France later in the summer, but she is hesitant. "I thought about it and thought, 'I can't go to France.' Too much ISIS and everybody. But someone reminded me I am 80 years old. If I'm ever gonna go, I should go now."

So Janet will check Saint Tropez off her list of surfisticated places to visit, but by September she and Steve will be back in Scorpion Bay—where the stars at night, are big and bright, and prime time for well-traveled south swells.

All the peace and quiet they can handle. Surfing, digging for shark's teeth and arrowheads, relaxing, reading, staying healthy, staying fit.

But this time they will be prepared. They bought a stingray kit at Walgreens and are taking it down to Mexico with them.

Pauline Ado somewhere on La Côte des Basques, fueling up with some high-octane espresso before paddling out to get some barrels
Photo: Lucia Griggi

Born: February 14, 1991
Birthplace: Hendaye, France

MUCH ADO ABOUT PAULINE

I have no idea what I would be doing if I wasn't surfing professionally. I wanted to be a pro surfer since I was 13. I don't think I have ever wanted to be anything else.

—*Pauline Ado*

QUEL DOMMAGE! QUEL FROMAGE!

Pauline Ado. *Qu'est-ce que c'est?*

She surfs for Rip Curl, and if you look at her profile on the ripcurl.com website, you will learn that she is 1.66 M and 59 kg—5'5" and 129.8 pounds to you and me. Pauline's home spot is Anglet, France. Her favorite spot is "Indo," which is a country and not a spot, but whatever. She surfs regular stance, which means her left foot is forward and she faces the wave going right. Her favorite surfer is Australian Joel Parkinson, her favorite maneuver is "tail slide," and her competitive achievements include ISA World Junior Champion in 2006, ASP World Junior Champion in 2008, and qualifier for the World Championship Tour in 2011.

When you check out her videos online you will see *Pauline à la plage 01*, and there is Pauline "playing the sexy card," as Matt Warshaw would say: all made up like a *Parisienne madame*, flicking her hair; giving off mean, sultry, not-a-chance looks; stripping down to a bathing suit and high heels; showing off her *derriere* to the world; making a gardener drool; then slipping off her high heels seductively and diving into the pool—seductively.

All of this is to that song from *Top Gun*.

Quel dommage! Quel fromage!

And then there is an abrupt cut to Pauline's face, close up.

Pauline cutting back in Hossegor, France, October 2014
Photo: Lucia Griggi

She says to the camera, in French: "Are we done with your crap? Can I go surf now?!"

Yeah, Pauline! Making an anti–sexism-in-surfing statement. Fooled us!

And then there's a minute or so of quick edits of Pauline surfing, showing off her other backside: backside thwacks to the lip, frontside carves, big power hooks, and pulling into the barrel.

Pauline Ado is 1.66 M and 59 kg of dyno-mite!

When you're done cracking up over *Pauline à la plage 01*, check out *Pauline Ado, Surfing at Home*. This is Pauline "surfing some fun waves in the southwest of France," which is Pauline's home corner of the world. This must have been mostly shot in summer, because Pauline is making mountains out of molehills—generating speed in small beach break and point surf. She can ride small waves and make it look good, but there are glimpses of her pulling into the barrel in some meatier overhead surf, and you get a taste of what Pauline is about. She is not a small-wave wizard. She grew up in the Bay of Biscay, surfing some of the best beach breaks in the world. Pauline craves *puissance.*

Now look at *Pauline Ado Surfing Bells Beach* and you'll see her in long, over-head surf at Bells Beach, Australia. This is what Pauline craves—long waves with power that allow her to stretch out all 5'5" of her and carve big turns and surf with *vitesse.*

She's funny. She rips. We like her. *Qui est Pauline Ado?*

LE COTE BASQUE

Pauline Ado is from Hendaye, France, very close to the Spanish border. Hendaye is equidistant from San Sebastian, Spain, and Biarritz, France, but in the middle of a curve of coast that offers a variety of surf from summer beach breaks to winter cloud breaks—two feet to 40 feet. According to Pauline, "Hendaye has a very safe beach."

Pauline taking to the waves in
Puerto Rico, November 2010
Photo: Lucia Griggi

"Are we done with
your crap? Can I
go surf now?!"

**Always a smile here
with Pauline at home in
France, March 2016**
Photo: Lucia Griggi

Growing up, she loved to spend time in the water, playing with her friends, who were mostly boys. They used to try to stand up, catching waves on their body boards. Eventually they asked their parents if they could start surfing, and they all went to the local surf club. Pauline was around 8, and she loved it from the beginning. After trying soccer, tennis, and handball, she started surfing and never stopped.

Her first board was a 6'0" made by a local shaper. She bought it from another girl surfer, and it had a big butterfly sprayed on it. "Very girly spray," Pauline remembered. "I didn't like the spray (because I was a bit of a tomboy) and the fact that it was so big at first. But the board was feeling good under my feet, so I changed my mind."

THAT OBSESSION

When surfing grabs a person, it can grab them pretty hard and become an obsession—sometimes a positive obsession, sometimes not. With Pauline, surfing became a family affair. Pauline's parents had never been surfers, but after she started, her parents and younger sister took it up too. Her parents didn't stick with it long, but her sister was pretty good. She used to compete and did some Pro Juniors. The two still sometimes go out surfing together.

Pauline was competitive with her sister, but she was inspired by two pro surfers who did well internationally: Marie-Pierre Abgrall and Emmanuelle Joly. "They were my idols, and I wanted to do like them."

Pauline taking to her home break, France 2014
Photo: Lucia Griggi

THAT WINNING FEELING

Pauline fell in love with surfing right off the bat, but she wasn't too sure about competition—at first. Her teachers pushed her to start competing, and she initially hated it. The conditions were poor, and she could never catch the minimum of three waves in 15 minutes. "It was frustrating."

But her teachers insisted she keep it up. Pauline won her first contest when she was 10 and got sponsored by Rip Curl. That changed her mind. "This was a huge boost. I thought competing wasn't bad after all. I liked that winning feeling and got into it. I kept on competing, and my results got better and better." Many times she was competing with surfers much older than she.

Pauline was 9 when she surfed in her first contest, but the French amateur surfing scene is well organized and coordinated with schools. French education is all about recognizing and nurturing talent, and with Pauline that talent was surfing. The French federation has deals with some schools so that students can finish early and train. "But a lot of times it's not enough, and that is where sponsors are a big part of your career." In Pauline's case it was Rip Curl, a wet suit and

**Silhouetted by spray, Pauline
charging at home in France, 2014**
Photo: Lucia Griggi

clothing manufacturer who saw her talent early and sponsored her at 10 years old. The team manager and her coach sent her everywhere for training and competing. "I wouldn't be where I am today without that."

SURF THE WORLD

Pauline took her surf trip to Morocco at 10 years old, and if you are thinking Morocco would seem *romantique et exotique et fantastique* to a 10-year-old surfer girl, well it was.

She surfed all over Europe—Spain, Portugal, Canary Islands.

For a teenager given the choice between traveling the world and surfing perfect waves with the world's best and sitting inside four walls in a stuffy classroom—well that wasn't much of a choice at all. "I was traveling a lot," Pauline said. "I would miss weeks of school. In the summer I would travel all around Europe for competing, and in the winter I would go to Hawaii, Australia, Bali . . . for training." Yet she still managed to do well in school because that was the deal with her parents: "As long as you're doing good at school, you can travel for surfing." Her own drive for success combined with amazing friends and family helped her successfully manage both school and surfing.

HERE TODAY, GONE TO TAHITI

At 13 years old, Pauline qualified for the French Junior team to compete in the ISA World Juniors (under age 18) in the French equivalent of Hawaii: Tahiti. It was the first time she saw the best surfers in the world and thought maybe she could be one of them in a few years. That trip put the travel and adventure bug into Pauline—as Tahiti does to most people—and she started thinking about being a pro surfer. Rip Curl was starting to push her to travel and compete around the world, so she went to Hawaii and spent time in Australia every winter.

At 15 years old, Pauline traveled to Maresias, Brazil, to compete at the ISA World Juniors. Surfing in punchy beach breaks, Pauline competed against future world beaters Courtney Conlogue and Sally Fitzgibbons—and beat them both. "Winning the ISA World Juniors at 15 was huge, and probably a surprise for most people," Pauline said. "Winning that event was one of my dreams, but maybe I wasn't expecting to win that title that young. I wasn't one of the favorites, and it was the first world title for France in surfing."

Pauline's life changed after winning the World Junior title in Brazil. The victory was a very big deal in France, but the world also began to take notice. She got more exposure and proved to her friends and family that she could do it—she could be a pro surfer if she worked hard enough. After that she began putting pressure on herself to perform in competition.

After her victory, Pauline continued to attend school, but she was often pulled away for competition and surf trips. She was never home for the holidays, always traveling and surfing. "After the title, Rip Curl took me on a boat trip to the Mentawai Islands with their international team: Steph Gilmore, Jessi Miley-Dyer, Alana Blanchard, and Bethany Hamilton. It was like a dream come true to go on a trip with them in such an amazing place for surfing. I learned so much."

GOING PRO

No more pencils, no more books, no more teachers' looks of envy. As soon as school was finished, Pauline turned pro. She had surfed in her first World Qualifying Series at 13, when she was given a wildcard into an event in France. "Waves were pretty big and I was scared, but I still went out and gave my best. It was intimidating but also a great motivation to surf against pros."

Pauline has been competing as a pro full-time since 2009. Take a look at the World Surf League website and you can see Pauline's competitive year broken down year by year, heat by heat. Asked about her proudest competitive moment, Pauline goes back to the beginning. "Probably (again) when I won the ISA's World Juniors in 2006. It's my best competitive memory. Being the first French [citizen] to achieve a world title was so exciting!"

She does best when the waves have a nice open face where she can throw all 5'5", 129.8 pounds of her into big, hooking carves. "That being said . . . I also love to get barreled!"

As a pro surfer, Pauline loves not having a routine and learning something every day from every trip, from all the different surfing conditions. She doesn't like time spent in airports, in airplanes, and in cars. Pauline likes to move.

Pauline paddling out in Hossegor,
France, April 2016
Photo: Lucia Griggi

Pauline heading toward the surf break
in Puerto Rico, November 2012
Photo: Lucia Griggi

PAULINE ON THE MOVE

During summer 2016, as this book was being written, Pauline was on the move. There were long gaps in her e-mail answers to questions, but when you look at her schedule, that was understandable.

Determined to surf her way back into the big leagues of the World Championship Tour, Pauline surfed twelve of the twenty-seven World Qualifying Series events held from January to September. In March/April, she won QS #11 at Zarautz, Spain. In the second week of September, she won QS #27 in Morocco. At the end of September, Pauline took a thirteenth in World Championship Tour event #13 in Portugal.

At the end of September 2016, Pauline was ranked #8 on the World Qualifying Series. With five events remaining in Costa Rica, Chile, Japan, and Australia, Pauline was looking good to make the WCT for 2017. E-mailing from the WCT event in Portugal, Pauline said. "I am having a good year but still need to perform at the end of the season if I want to achieve my goals."

Pauline's goals as a surfer are to improve in the innovation area, be able to pull out new turns, and work on giving her 100 percent in every event. As a person, Pauline wants "to be more and more able to enjoy every little moment from every situation. Live the present to its fullest!"

Pauline intends to compete for a few more years, as long as the motivation is still there. "I love to surf and compete. As long as I have that, I might just keep on! But who knows what can happen in life? After surfing I am still not sure what I will do. It's something I think about a lot, but I'm still undecided."

PAULINE À LA PLAGE

And after that? Maybe Pauline Ado will find a second career as a rebel French filmmaker, along the lines of Francois Truffaut, Jean-Luc Godard, Louis Malle, Alice Guy, or Agnes Jaoui.

Pauline Ado made some waves with her anti-sexism statement *Pauline à la plage 01*. Where did that come from, and is there more? "It all started from a funny conversation about how women's surfing is portrayed sometimes," Pauline said. "I think it's great to promote women's surfing in a glamorous way, but a few times it's pushed way too far. We shot the clip in Costa Rica last summer (2015)."

What was the reaction? "People were pretty surprised," Pauline said. "People that know me were very amused. Some big media [outlets] talked about it in France. It was just a funny way to talk about a more serious subject."

Pauline Ado, looking *très chic* as she hits the slip somewhere cold
Photo: Lucia Griggi

SOURCES

Mahalo to Tonya Bickerton Watson for her *kokua*, attention to detail, and speed and efficacy.

INTRODUCTION
All the quotes about getting injured at Teahupoo come from "Keala Kennelly: 'It Swallowed Me Whole,' Kauaian charger talks massive Teahupoo tube," an interview with Janna Irons, posted July 30, 2015: surfermag.com/features/ keala-kennelly-it-swallowed-me-whole/#yPsQThLXjmjJqxeV.97.

ROCHELLE BALLARD
Lessa, Christina. *Women Who Win*. Milford, CT: Universe Publishing Company, October 15, 1998.

Matt Warshaw's quote about Rochelle Ballard from *The Encyclopedia of Surfing*: encyclopediaofsurfing.com/entries/ballard-rochelle.

Gina Mackin's 2000 quote from Rochelle Ballard in Matt Warshaw's *Encyclopedia of Surfing*: encyclopediaofsurfing.com/entries/ballard-rochelle.

Rochelle Ballard's injury during the shooting of *Blue Crush* from "The Price of Gas" by Ben Marcus in *The Surfer's Journal*, volume 12(2): surfersjournal.com/ product/the-price-of-gas.

BETHANY HAMILTON
Kelly Slater's Instagram quote about Bethany from @kellyslater.

Hamilton, Bethany, and Rick Bundschuh, with Sheryl Berk. *Soul Surfer: A True Story of Faith Family and Fighting to Get Back on the Board*. New York: MTV Books; reprint edition, June 26, 2012.

Matt Warshaw's quotes about Bethany from *The Encyclopedia of Surfing*: encyclopediaofsurfing.com/entries/hamilton-bethany.

Bethany's quote on faith from her website: bethanyhamilton.com/faith.

Quote on NSSA Nationals 2004 from "2004 NSSA Nationals Wrap Up" on surfer mag.com, posted July 22, 2010: surfermag.com/features/o4nssanat/#OXEHHy WKzgiza58X.99.

"Bethany Does It!" quote from "2005 NSSA National Championships Results": nssa .org/newsmanager/templates/NSSAArticle.aspx?articleid=142&zoneid=8.

Timeline of Bethany's life from bethanyhamilton.com/category/timeline.

MAYA GABEIRA

Maya's quotes from Red Bull's documentary *Watch Maya Gabeira on the Long Road Back to Nazaré*: redbull.com/us/en/surfing/stories/1331795089375/maya-gabeira-return-to-nazare-red-bull-tv-documentary.

Matt Skenazy's quotes on Maya Gabeira from "Maya Takes a Breath," posted September 3, 2014: outsideonline.com/1925936/maya-gabeira-takes-breath.

Laird Hamilton's quote on Maya Gabeira on CNN: youtube.com/watch?v=azYk-98xtrw.

Greg Long's quote on Maya Gabeira from Matt Skenazy's "Maya Takes a Breath," posted September 3, 2014: outsideonline.com/1925936/maya-gabeira-takes-breath.

Quote about Fernando Gabeira as the "rock and roll politician" and the use of thong bikinis for men at Ipanema from "Fernando Gabeira" on the *Lost Sambista* blog: lostsambablog.com/2012/11/20/1282.

Maya's quote about her dad being tough and other quotes from Susan Casey's "Maya Gabeira: The Girl Who Will Surf Anything," posted November 3, 2008: womenshealthmag.com/fitness/maya-gabeira-interview.

Carlee Wallace's quote on Maya Gabeira from "Surfer Maya Gabeira: Beyond the Blue," posted March 8, 2015: info.lululemon.com/features/up-close-and-personal/maya-gabeira.

Matt Warshaw's description of Maya Gabeira from *The Encyclopedia of Surfing*: encyclopediaofsurfing.com/entries/gabeira-maya.

KEALA KENNELLY

Matt George's quote on Keala Kennelly from "Keala Kennelly—The Naked Truth," posted July 22, 2010: surfermag.com/features/keala/#spvoOR1fxjPE3gVX.97.

Keala's quotes about Andy and Bruce Irons and other quotes from "Chasing the Swell: An Interview with Surfer Keala Kennelly" by Laia Garcia, posted November 11, 2015: lennyletter.com/culture/interviews/a152/chasing-the-swell-an-interview-with-surfer-keala-kennelly.

Matt Warshaw's quotes on Keala Kennelly from *The Encyclopedia of Surfing*: encyclopediaofsurfing.com/entries/kennelly-keala.

Keala tow surfing Teahupoo in 2005 from "2005 Billabong Pro Tahiti: Pre Event," posted by *Surfing* magazine, May 3, 2005: surfingmagazine.com/news/tahiti_050305/#7jA2Tgveggj1X0cM.97.

Keala's quote on towing Jaws from *KEALA KENNELLY RECOUNTS HER FIRST TOW SESSION AT JAWS* posted December 19, 2009: www.surfermag.com/features/keala-kennelly-recounts-her-first-tow-session-at-jaws/#yf63mpO-BEtAaKVoy.99.

Keala's quote on the Nelscott contest from "Keala Kennelly on Winning Big" by Janna Irons, posted November 19, 2010: surfermag.com/features/keala -kennelly-on-winning-big/#8eaZKtWr6fDxwVZ1.99.

Keala's quote to Joe Turpel from "Interview: Keala Kennelly, KK on her horrific injury after an average wipeout at small Teahupoo," posted September 13, 2011: surfline.com/surf-news/interview-keala-kennelly_59360.

ANDREA MOLLER

Matt Warshaw's definition of "waterman" from *The Encyclopedia of Surfing*: encyclopediaofsurfing.com/entries/waterman.

Andrea's quotes to Anna Dimond from "Andrea Moller: Let's Join the Big-Wave Party" by Anna Dimond, posted February 19, 2016: worldsurfleague.com/posts/ 181460/andrea-moller-on-women-in-big-wave-we-want-to-join-the-party.

Andrea's quotes to Matt Chebatoris in "From Big Waves to Big Winds, Andrea Moller Masters All," posted April 26, 2016: supexaminer.com/2016/04/from- big-waves-to-big-winds-andrea-moller-masters-all/#.WCZCotUrLC0.

Andrea's quotes from the 2016 XXL Big Wave Awards: youtube.com/watch? v=yjbQGU_OkHo.

LEAH DAWSON

Definition of "soul surfer" from *The Encyclopedia of Surfing*: encyclopediaof surfing.com/entries/soul-surfer.

The quote from the 3:54 edit of Leah Dawson surfing is from *Leah Dawson Might Save Women's Surfing*, posted November 10, 2015, by Zach Weisberg: the inertia.com/creators/leah-dawson-might-save-womens-surfing.

Leah's quote about yoga with Anna Langer for *Pro Chat* on CoolerLifestyle.com, posted April 19, 2013: https://coolerlifestyle.com/features/pro-chat-leah- dawson.html.

Leah's quote on The Sea Appreciation Project from "Hi-Fives with Leah Dawson" with Teton Gravity Research, posted July 9, 2013: tetongravity.com/story/ surf/Hi-Fiveswith-Leah-Dawson-6538510.

Leah's thoughts on the marketing of women surfers with Aeriel Brown on read wax.com: readwax.com/leah-dawson.

ALANA BLANCHARD

Haddid, S. (2013, August 19). *The Inertia*. Retrieved from www.theinertia.com/surf/ alana-blanchard-profile-carte. Editor's Note: This article was first published by *Cooler* magazine here: https://coolerlifestyle.com/features/carte-blanchard .html.

Kerry, C. (2014, February 19). Alana Blanchard: Surfing, sexuality, and 1.6m fans, photos. *Newcastle Herald*. Retrieved from http://www.theherald.com.au/story/2100755/alana-blanchard-surfing-sexuality-and-16m-fans-photos.

Melekian, B. (2014, January 14). Alana Blanchard. *Surfer Magazine*. Retrieved from http://www.surfermag.com/features/alana-blanchard/#RSlyOo6WUubSDjRy.97.

Networka.com (Producer). (n.d.). *Alana: Surfer girl* [Television series]. Network A. www.networka.com/shows/2/alana-surfer-girl.

Warshaw, M. (n.d.). "Blanchard Alana," in *Encyclopedia of Surfing* by Matt Warshaw. Retrieved December 17, 2016, from http://encyclopediaofsurfing.com/entries/blanchard-alana.

BIANCA VALENTI

Bianca's interview with Justin Housman, "Big Wave Bianca," posted February 5, 2015: surfermag.com/features/bianca-valenti/#W7alBXHEI3faiKAQ.97.

PAIGE ALMS

Paige's quote about the barrel at Jaws from the video *Paige Alms' Barrel at Jaws*: youtube.com/watch?v=stR1vmxf1As.

Paige's quote about loving bigger waves from "Ripple Effect: How Paige Alms Is Taking Female Big-Wave Surfing to New Heights," from an interview with Will Coldwell posted on *The Guardian* on October 14, 2015: theguardian.com/travel/2015/oct/14/paige-alms-female-big-wave-surfing-new-heights.

Paige's quote about wiping out in Mexico, big wave training, and breath holding from an interview in *FreeSurf* magazine: freesurfmagazine.com/paige-alms.

ALISON TEAL

Alison's snake-kissing story from "Snaked!" on her personal website: alisons adventures.com/films/snaked.

SALLY FITZGIBBONS

Sally's quotes to Chris Roots from "The Day Sally Fitzgibbons Ditched Athletics for Surfing," posted February 3, 2008: illawarramercury.com.au/story/604006/the-day-sally-fitzgibbons-ditched-athletics-for-surfing.

Matt Warshaw's description of Sally Fitzgibbons from *The Encyclopedia of Surfing*: encyclopediaofsurfing.com/entries/fitzgibbons-sally.

Sally describing her win at Bells to Justin Cote in "Sally Fitzgibbons Wins the 2011 Rip Curl Pro Bells Beach," posted April 23, 2011: grindtv.com/surf/sally-fitzgibbons-wins-the-2011-rip-curl-pro-bells-beach/#Gp1AktHs27IE4BO1.97.

Sally's quote about the World Title in an interview with Janna Irons from "The World Title Battle: Carissa vs. Sally, Women's World Title Comes Down to Biarritz and Huntington," posted July 7, 2011: surfermag.com/features/the-world-title-battle-carissa-vs-sally/#JI0R6auMRGjs4cSz.99.

Sally's quotes about fitness knowledge and training from her website: sally fitzgibbons.com.

ROSY HODGE

Derek Reilly getting excited about Rosy Hodge from "The Daring Adventures of Rosy Hodge," posted July, 2016 in *Stab* magazine: stabmag.com/girls/the-daring-adventures-of-rosy-hodge.

Rosy's quote about her shark encounter from "Two Top Professional SA Surfers Survive Radical Shark Encounter in East London on Saturday," with Craig Jarvis, posted May 28, 2010: indosurflife.com/2010/05/two-top-professional-sa-surfers-survive-radical-shark-encounter-in-east-london-on-saturday.

JANET MACPHERSON

Jamie Brisick's quotes about Janet and Sean Macpherson from "Room for Two," *Surfer's Journal* 23(2): surfersjournal.com/product/room-for-two.

Princess Ka'iulani being described as "the daughter of a double race," from the Robert Louis Stevenson poem "To Princess Kaiulani" in *Songs of Travel* (1896): poetryloverspage.com/poets/stevenson/to_princess_kaiulani.html.

Sean Macpherson's quote about The Maritime hotel from "One on One with Sean Macpherson," posted October 15, 2015, in *Haute Living*: hauteliving.com/2015/10/one-on-one-with-sean-macpherson/589630.

PAULINE ADO

Pauline à la plage 01: https://vimeo.com/143240702.

INDEX

ABOUT THE AUTHORS

Ben Marcus served as editor of *Surfer* magazine for ten years, where he wrote the first story on Mavericks, inaugurated the Surfer Magazine Surf Video Awards, and oversaw exciting years in the evolution of surfing. After leaving *Surfer*, Ben took to the road as a wandering writer and worked on many books covering a variety of topics. Ben has also done extensive writing for magazines and newspapers: the *LA Times*, *LA Weekly*, *Malibu Magazine*, *Men's Journal*, *Outside*, *Fly Fish Journal*, *Standup Journal*, *The Surfer's Journal*, and others. Ben currently lives in Hawaii on a 15-meter utility boat in Kewalo Basin Harbor.

Lucia Griggi is a world-traveling photographer specializing in the surfing, skateboarding, and outdoor adventure world. Lucia focuses on lifestyle and adventure for editorial and advertising clients. Some of her clients include National Geographic, ESPN, Red Bull, Sri Lankan Airlines, BBC, Land Rover, Patagonia, and Jeep. In her photography, Lucia mixes her passions for travel, people, and adventure. Lucia's work has been internationally recognized and awarded by National Geographic, PDN, Windland Smith Rice International Awards, Black and White photography, and the Masters Cup. When not shooting, Lucia can be found surfing the Californian coastline or visiting family back home in England. Lucia has collaborated with Ben Marcus on *Skateboard: The Good, the Rad and the Gnarly*; *365 Surfboards*; and *The Art of Stand Up Paddling*.